In the criminal's cabinet
An nthology of poetry and fiction

Edited by Val Stevenson & Todd Swift

nthposition press
London, England

First published in 2004 by nthposition press

British Library Cataloguing in Progress Data
A catalogue record for this book is available from the British Library

ISBN 0954626818

Cover image: Alex Severin, based on
In the criminal's cabinet, Holmes discovers himself',
by Jason Camlot
Art direction: Etienne Gilfillan
Production: Neil Mortimer
Typeset in Swift and Trebuchet
Cover printed by Avon Printing
Printed and bound in England by Antony Rowe Ltd.

nthposition press
38 Allcroft Road
London NW5 4NE
www.nthposition.com

We gratefully acknowledge the Arts Council's assistance in funding this book.

Acknowledgements

Thanks to Sarah Blair, Neil Mortimer and Ariadne van de Ven for their invaluable advice and assistance. Charles Beckett and Kate Griffin at the Arts Council went out of their way to be helpful. Sara Egan and Paul Sieveking put up with *nthposition*'s demands on their partners' time. Thanks to the nthposition contributors, both those included here and those we couldn't squeeze in, for their support over the last two years. And thanks, last but most certainly not least, to the *nthposition* subscribers who made this book possible: Bruce Barkman, Baz Hurrell, Tom Bradley, Dan Britten, Peter Cavaye, Patrick Chapman, David Clarke, Laura Cowan, Christopher de Coulon Berthoud, Sarah Ereira, Barbara Fletcher, Guy Herron, Celia Mitchell, Paul Music, Joe Palmer, Eileen Patskin, Judith Rycar, June Shenfield, Harry and Paddy Stevenson, Seamus Sweeney, Roisin Tierney and Pierre Wassenaar. We appreciate your faith in the project.

Val Stevenson & Todd Swift

Contents

Introduction 1

If this were the last sonnet in my life *Robert Allen* 3
Boston bar New Year's *Tammy Armstrong* 4
Alayan cyborg *Louise Bak* 5
Many mansions *Carole Baldock* 7
Fusing the braids *Simon Barraclough* 9
Shooting pigeons with your fingers *Jim Bennett* 10
Fig 4 *Caroline Bergvall* 12
Memories *Charles Bernstein* 13
th system is nervus *bill bissett* 15
The continent *Stephanie Bolster* 16
Harsh words of mercury *Tom Bradley* 17
Earthenware more porous than metal,
    absorbs particles of the flesh *Kimberly Burwick* 26
In the criminal's cabinet, Holmes
    discovers himself *Jason Camlot* 27
Bring up a child in the way he
    should go *Sherry Chandler* 28
[the return of the ring] *Maxine Chernoff* 29
Farmy *Todd Colby* 31
The fitness of the human heart *MTC Cronin* 32
The internal life of a brick *Kieran D'Angelo* 33
Sheep on hill pasture *Robert Davidson* 49
Theater *Jennifer K Dick* 50
Life model *Andrew Dilger* 51
Black cowboy hat *BR Dionysius* 52
Gemini *Isobel Dixon* 53
Flea circus *Antony Dunn* 55
Blood of a mole *Zdravka Evtimova* 56
Italian masturbazione *Peter Finch* 59
Memorial *David Finkle* 60
Coffee *Martin Fisher* 85

The blood cycle	*Brentley Frazer*	94
A textbook case	*Philip Fried*	98
After sex, the news	*Ethan Gilsdorf*	100
The cigarette	*John Goodby*	101
Cold capital	*Giles Goodland*	102
pilot light	*Daphne Gottlieb*	105
The red line	*Carrie Haber*	106
Pelicans at the weir, Saskatoon	*Jen Hadfield*	110
Modern Maid	*Christine Hamm*	111
The river is far behind us	*Paul Hardacre*	112
No better a house	*Kenneth J Harvey*	115
Address book	*Steven Heighton*	124
November	*Kevin Higgins*	126
Poetics	*Paul Hoover*	127
The Orientalist	*Ranjit Hoskote*	128
At the roadblock	*Halvard Johnson*	129
Up there	*Fred Johnston*	130
Garden	*Jill Jones*	131
Serir	*Norman Jope*	132
Wasp	*Jayne Fenton Keane*	133
a mother instead	*WB Keckler*	135
Sex in the confines	*Amy King*	136
Boxing gloves	*Chris Kinsey*	137
Sorry	*Roddy Lumsden*	138
A tale of two Sickerts	*Alexis Lykiard*	139
Enough of apple picking now	*Don McGrath*	141
Terzanelle for a killing	*Nigel McLoughlin*	142
Asylum seeker	*Jo Mazelis*	143
From the intestines of a mystical dog	*Valeria Melchioretto*	144
Sprinkler	*Matthew Miller*	145
Narration	*Vivek Narayanan*	146
Left untitled in the ensuing melee (*titre provisoire*)	*Michelle Noteboom*	149
A writer's life	*Nessa O'Mahony*	150
It's gonna take a lotta love; or, God bless the conspiracy	*Richard Peabody*	151
Stop the war or giant amœbas will eat you	*Richard Peabody*	154
Burning Omaha	*Tom Phillips*	170
kyoto crow(s)	*David Prater*	171
Kernel	*Sina Queyras*	172

Carthage	*Srikanth Reddy*	173
"If you think they don't go crazy in tiny rooms"	*Ali Riley*	174
A cold room in Granada	*Peter Riley*	177
Facing death	*Peter Robinson*	178
a bed between summer and fall	*Noel Rooney*	179
Listen up	*Thaddeus Rutkowski*	180
Apache tears	*Rebecca Seiferle*	181
The decline of the beetle empire	*John W Sexton*	182
Dadaquest	*Ron Silliman*	183
Taking your fun while you can	*Hal Sirowitz*	186
Eight forty five am	*Hank Starrs*	187
The sacrifice	*Sean Street*	188
The waxwing slain	*Seamus Sweeney*	190
exile	*Joel Barraquiel Tan*	198
Scars	*Heather Taylor*	200
Half mile down	*Roisin Tierney*	201
To leveling swerve	*Rodrigo Toscano*	202
Killing fields	*Ilija Trojanow*	205
Pupil	*Alison Trower*	206
The daisy. The dolphin. The dagger. The dragon	*Paul Vermeersch*	207
Travel	*John Welch*	208
Poets	*John Hartley Williams*	209
Work ethic	*Philip Wilson*	213
An education	*Max Winter*	214
Landscape	*Harriet Zinnes*	215
Contributors		217

Introduction

What is written online is writ on electric water; it cannot shift units even as it reaches millions of hits. This book is the product of an ironic inversion: a digital presence, which is at once ubiquitous and potentially ephemeral, being transformed into an inscribed and bound form. What has made *nthposition* so popular has been its mode of dissemination: free, to everyone with access to the web. We no longer need to be told that online publication is as "authentic" as print; however, there is a curious, traditional validation that occurs when online work is returned to the nostalgic retro-mode of paper.

Since 2002, London-based *nthposition* has featured several hundred poets, from almost every place where people write poetry in English, especially America, Australia, Canada, India, Ireland, New Zealand, the UK and South Africa. Our ebooks (such as *100 poets against the war*) have been downloaded tens of thousands of times. Macmillan's *Writer's Handbook 2005* has grouped the site with *Jacket* and a handful of others as among the world's best for poetry. By selecting over 80 poets to represent the many more (and equally fine) who have been showcased at *nthposition*, we have tried to offer a full-spectrum report on the state of poetry of the start of the 21st century, to suggest the various ways – from linguistically innovative to mainstream – a poem can be imagined and created. Good poems occur at all points of the writing compass, from political to just plain weird.

Within these pages, you will find, quite simply, indelible poets and poems to reckon with – from India's Ranjit Hoskote to Ireland's Kevin Higgins; from Canada's Stephanie Bolster to the UK's Jen Hadfield; from America's Charles Bernstein to South Africa's Isobel Dixon...

As with the poetry, we have avoided the thematic and generic shackles of many anthologies in selecting the fiction. The final choice was almost arbitrary: how do you choose between social comedy and small tragedies, pitch-black social commentary and gothic fantasy? The nine selected writers go some way towards showing the range of fiction submitted to *nthposition*. The writers come from the UK, America, Canada, Ireland, Bulgaria and Japan; live in inner cities and the countryside; and write seriously and amusingly. All write tight, vivid prose.

Enjoy it.

Val Stevenson & Todd Swift

If this were the last sonnet in my life

Robert Allen

Just fourteen lines? Shakespeare set upon his task
one summer day in 1592. He had fled the plague, but
was young, in his early twenties probably, before

the histories and tragedies had played out in his head
and made him brittle with things he didn't want
to know. Of course he was just making a living,

as I am now, with the cheat of useless lyrics
like an afternoon of half-meant words and flirtatious
conversation. The moon is now in its first quarter,

identical to the one he saw low in the trees, as he wrote
lines by candle light. I have around eighty to go
before I catch him, but the sky throws lines like dice:

the last sonnet I will ever write. It is wildly imperfect,
and halts like a gallery ghost at fourteen lines.

Boston bar New Year's

Tammy Armstrong

Another year tunneling
through a tail bone of ice
suspended off the Coquihalla:
elk crossings, cougar tramped paths
bonfire blisters mudding all that white.

This is where New Year's begins
where shadowed faces shimmy
caldera star diluvium
for a countdown, a disposition that says
tear here, begin again.

In a cabin, the groundskeeper sighs rum
while lost dogs sleep
around his margin of bedding
pricking up for voices beyond the creek
cat spat of opened beers
ten, nine, eight...

Beyond the bark shorn sumacs:
no one to contend with
no one to peel back a sheer drape
to find the howler on their own front lawn
feet deep in a recycling crate
head thrown toward heaven
challenging the new year coming down
burning up before the impact.

Alayan cyborg

Louise Bak

our eyes are tide-tugged up the peak to the hailing figures,
down to the trough of the honorable, despairing elder.
the recumbent post-acting porn star is in the front left,
drawing the scarlet damask on the cart, through the
mirroring at the water's edge.

he embraced her, but what he felt beneath her light coat
was no more than the firmness of her tightly-wound *obi*,
with its padded layers and its huge bow. he raised a
Sakaki branch and waved it over her head. its paper
pendants flashed a pure white rubedo on her cheek.
their silence was that of a number of small rabbits,
each holding its breath within the shelter of its own
lusty Belsen thicket.
is love supposed to glow on like this after the set has been
switched off? he ran his hands nervously through his hair
and suddenly faced the beam of a flashlight. he felt fear,
squeaking between the pressure of his fingertips. rearing
her head from his chest, deftly *tabi*-shod, she moved in tip-toe.
a purposelessness of a *Taisho*-era swoon, her glaived-bust
bulged with electrons, and her sesamoid cells split
into cubic heaps. she was drooping from the bye-bye in
the sweat saturated air.
her father ripped off his *kendo* mask. his lips formed a line
as straight as a sword, and the *waki* arose with plastic vacuoles,
bursting orgies of flowers. they expect it to crumble into sticky
powdered sugar, but when the knife makes contact, it scrapes
but does not give. though she pulls at it,
the surrounding tissue doesn't move. People's eyes were
moist, watching as her skin shone like vinaigrette dressing.

on the monitor, a digital marigold quivered a sincerer gold
in its pot. the director yelled cut, as he pulled the flesh away,
we could see the heart was not connected to a thing. guard
cells were bursting to prop open her stomatas for maximum
oxygen flow, so she could utter her last gasp. she sucked in

6

a saliva packet and burst it
before the official flashlight and bonds were waved again.
noticing with a blurred eye that one of the group was
flurried, she touched her lips to his, as to feel their texture
clearly. the lofty deck on the crane bristled with a sniper.
a kind of shyness kept him from daring to tell her that
each man would undertake his mission with a petal of her
alaya hidden upon him. the tropical light was like hundreds
of massed spearheads of
marshalled troops, on her again. he licked the glucose pools
under her eyes as her erotonide chip jabbed through her outer
cells and glowed like fired wire. if we only we knew the film's
real special effect lied, in signalling the action of him, accepting her,
on lips, that had yet touched no other.

Notes

alaya is a concept paired with a kind of awareness that nothing within the universe
truly possesses its own substance. Theories around this concept grew rather numerous, "the one hundred thousand diverse exegeses" that characterized Buddhism.
Another theory suggests that alaya consciousness was half-defiled, half-undefiled,
and hence could serve as the bridge to human salvation.
rubedo, redden, reddening, results from the fire's most intense heat.
Taisho era was a brief period in Japanese history when a whole-hearted surrender
to the emotions enjoyed favour. This earnest passion has now something of an anachronism that has become something to provoke laughter.
waki, Japanese priest.

Many mansions

Carole Baldock

Security is tight in the Hall,
all doors manned,
guests ushered,
well looked after,
watched over.

You mind your manners
in the Hall,
where windows soar
floor to ceiling,
letting in light,
but not heat.

Outside the Hall,
sun sweeps the plaza –
or is it piazza?
Crystal fountains,
gleaming sculptures
and tactful seats.

Inside the Hall,
MGM staircases swoop,
every floor deadened
with dense carpet.
Galleries, lavatories,
pristine; it's immaculate.

And the food?
Naturellement, exquisite,
picturesque on heavy plates,
water and juice in stem glasses.
All those serving
have such charming accents.

We are gathered together
in the Hall
to shake our heads
over those who despise Culture,
to consider how best
to help those wary of Culture.

Quite a conundrum.
What can we do?

How to prevent a flagship from
sinking,
preserve a showcase from
splintering.

Fusing the braids

Simon Barraclough

Three times a year you overhauled your hair,
firing the helical fuse that transformed
tightly raked rows into electrical storms
of static and dandruff and ionised air.
Then, your black nimbus would radiate past
the edges of photos, pillows on beds,
reducing your face to a shrunken head,
making you 'other', untethered, distressed.
So, for a weekend, I became taboo,
while expert fingers, with love, rebraided
the separate, warring strands within you,
so I could return, all conflict evaded,
to pass a candle flame from tip to tip,
fusing hair and plastic, lip upon lip.

Shooting pigeons with your fingers

Jim Bennett

in 1964 Billy Blackstock
fingers held like a gun
was playing at shooting pigeons
as he shouted "BANG"
a pigeon fell down dead

I saw Billy last week
and like every other time since then
he points his finger
like a gun and shouts "Bang"
and just like every other time
I say "Glad your aim's no better"
and somewhere in the chat
we talked about that bloody bird
again

I realized then that he has been
trying to fire his finger now
for over forty years

another guy I know
once found three half crowns
wrapped up in a five pound note
spoke about his good fortune
long after the money was spent
and ever since kicks at
paper and moves pavement rubbish
with his toe.
worse perhaps
he walks head down
scouring pavements
just ahead
for the tell tale signs
of treasure
he thinks he is the luckiest guy on earth
finding pennies most days
and always telling people

how lucky he is
I'm glad I never shot a pigeon
with my finger
or found a treasure trove
on a pavement
I don't think I could stand
the pressure

me I wrote a poem for my mum
she loved it
showed it to all her friends
for all the years before her death
would tell of how
I once wrote a poem for her

that was years ago
and I often think how odd it is
that a moment
years before can echo through a life

Fig 4

Caroline Bergvall

Fig 4 is a pattern.
A verification of means and of measure
as in safeguard.
Fear works against.
What gets applied follows recognition.
Being recognised as a part to play.
Misrecognised generates the most dedication.
A second glance requires more time.
In this way, there is much movement
yet little motion and many ways
to let rip are laid out not seen.
Language takes on where memory won't stick.
Simplifying to remember not
to deny
a feel for fruit
a touch of fruit.
No-place called home
nor home from home.
Yet not as divided as might first be assumed.
Invested proximity
makes clear a new citizenry.
Temporary subject to broken rule.
Homegrown buried shame with invitation.
Nor as separate.
Assemble to disperse.
Ghosting a range of activities
such as writing, eating, fucking.
For a while, I feel nothing I think nothing.
Held securely is not a bad position to be in.
Has many holdings
some to store.
Things will move accordingly.

Memories

Charles Bernstein

1 Grandfathers

The farm never seemed the same after gramps died
Grace kept saying, "Every life has its tide"
But to have his testicles cut that way
Even if he had done what, whatever they say

The corn grew high as a boy in britches
I loved the smell of the bulls and bitches
Motorcars and kikes seemed a world away
We thought we would always lounge in the hay

The first time I was in Kansas City
All the boys and girls looked so damn pretty
I said to my great friend, hey Joe, I said
How come gramps said we'd be better off dead

Than drinkin' the sweet liquor and tasting
              the fruits –
The muscles and turnips and duckling soups
Such that we never ever none did had
When, oh when, we were tiny lads

2 Heritage

Don't you steal that flag, my Mama had qualms
But a boy gotta have something to boast on
Crack that rock, slit that toad
Nature's a hoot if you shoot your load

Flies in the oven
Flies in the head
I'll kill that fly
Till I kill it dead
And no more will that fly
Bother me
As I roam and I ramble
In the tumbleweed

3 Tough love

My Dad and I were very close
I like to say, int'mately gruff:
We hunted bear, skinned slithy toes
You know, played ball and all that stuff.
Daddy had his pride and maybe was aloof
But when he hit me, that was proof –
Proof that he cared
More than he could ever share.
How I hated those men who took him away!
Pop was a passionate man
Just like me
And I'll teach my son, Clem
To love just like we men.

4 Sisters

William Kennedy Smith
He is an honorable man
And Mike Tyson's
A giant in my clan.
The liberals and the fem'nists
Hate men and vivisectionists.
But when they want the garbage out
Who do they ask, we guys no doubt.

th system is nervus

bill bissett

is th system sew nervus

th central nervus system is
veree sympathetik xcellent

have yu bin looking at th
evning sky its sew veree
beautiful   espeshulee

aftr running n swimming
with yu   running my
tongue all ovr yu thru

our mouths   evreething
we long 4 n dreem uv
liquid dreems thru our

beings merging 4 a whil
with each othr what we
want 2 having or not
we can go sew far astray
without climb in heer

2 bothr th othrwize
singul n separate we
loos our distansing
engayge n honour each
othrs flesh minds souls
being taste th rain n

feel all th heet cum
our endocreen empa
theez bathe in each
othr sighs n murmurs th
glandular swellings all
ovr enveloping feel

our greefs joys needs

The continent

Stephanie Bolster

In the train stations of the mind
someone is waiting under the arched roof.
Someone is ticking. Numbers shiver
on panels, trains drag out: TGV, Eurostar,
clackety, steam. Passengers rise on escalators
or clamber down stairs and aren't seen for days.
Sometimes as it's pulling out the beloved
grasps the door handle too late.
For that's who's waiting: the wished-for one.
Legs crossed, on the edge of a seat, watching
the display and the range of passing faces
for yours. But you are in another station.

Harsh words of mercury

Tom Bradley

Pity the Japanese woman who thinks bleak thoughts every time silvery water presents itself to her eye. She's like a sparrow reminded of steel wool when it bellies into a cloud.

Sui-gin, "water silver": the imagistic way her native tongue denoted a certain substance. She'd long since forgotten the term for it in Russian (probably an English cognate). This heavy, shiny, rolling gunk was like no other liquid her kindergarten classmates had ever run between their fingers and fondled in palms with all the scrapes, vermin bites and unnamed sores of active, normal, marginally-nourished Soviet childhood.

And among the pink hands were a few yellow ones, equally permeable. One pair belonged to an embassy brat with a large number of air miles already under her belt, a girl from an isle of bourgeois capitalism in the seas beyond Siberia. Her hands, in retrospect, were even scrawnier than those which would almost bungle the elementary school entrance examination a year later, back in Tokyo. Little Masako was a hyper-adrenalised nail biter even at that tender age, so there was no shortage of exposed quick and peeled-back hangnails on her microscopic fingertips. Plenty of holes and lesions for the juicy metal to seep into.

Their instructor, one Comrade Svidrigailov, was a gigantic snow-colored person, a failed applicant for admission to the Central Institute for Advanced Technology. She wanted her young charges never to be frustrated as she'd been. When not seated at the 12-ton cast-iron spinet accompanying unsyncopated songs in minor keys (nothing like the dozens of happy-go-lucky Portuguese ditties Masako had memorised in her Brasilia nursery school), Comrade Svidrigailov concentrated on providing the children with an intensive introduction to the wonders of science. She called it her modest contribution to the arms race with America, then in full swing.

She'd already demonstrated the phenomenal effects of liquid nitrogen: a downright circus of rubber balls exploding like light bulbs, whole reams of construction paper shattering like so many panes of glass, nails being hammered deep into concrete with the help of roughly cylindrical food items (which reconstituted themselves in Masako's memory as overripe bananas, but had probably been large barrel-pickled turnips). The whole extravaganza had been a major success, eliciting the only response Comrade Svidrigailov had ever gotten from the natty scions of rich party muckamucks in the front row. A few eyelids had even stirred among the otherwise feral communards and hereditary muzhiks in the back.

Aberrant substances seeming to get through to young minds where the mere language of Pushkin failed, Comrade Svidrigailov decided to try a similar approach again. Hydrochloric acid was her dream, for it would lead into many edifying discussions of the human digestive system, not to mention the intimidation techniques of gangsters in capitalist countries. But sulfuric acid was hard to come by, unlike her second choice of substances. And her second choice, as far as she was aware, was a lot less hazardous to handle.

So she used a change for the worse in the already terrible weather as a heavy-handed segue to a new topic in the science unit. She brought in a couple of baby thermometers, the intrusive occidental style. Not forgetting to field and pitch the expected jokes about the glass knob on the business end (Bolsheviks seemed to find in anuses a much richer source of humor than do Japanese – or at least Japanese of the governing class), she broke them open and, placing a dab on each little desk, invited the children to "get familiar" with the contents.

Warming to the occasion with the first hoots of ecstasy from the front row, Comrade Svidrigailov climbed on top of her own desk and revealed the dazzling way the nectar under consideration splashed and splintered into a million eyeball-grazing globules when allowed to drop from a height.

"But watch out for the broken glass. It's dangerous."

Masako hesitated to handle the stuff. It seemed not to belong within her range of experience, this liquid that hefted like a solid. A native of relatively balmy Honshu Island, she was still sorting out the relationship between the hard slippery material that clogged Moscow's gutters and the burning clouds that belched from the omnipresent samovars. But she allowed herself to be peer-pressured into participating in this "science project" because she thought it might be a good way to do what she was always urged to do by her mom, a former stewardess with Air France, where they'd mis-nicknamed her "China Doll" and printed her name tags accordingly for the decade-plus she'd flown with them.

"Find what it is about yourself," Mom said, "that might incite confusion or disharmonious feelings, and smooth it over." Open yourself wide like a lotus blossom and smile as you assimilate whatever metals they feel like forcing into your body.

Father must not have listened to such admonitions. After putting in more than a month of overtime, when he didn't get home at his usual hour of eleven o'clock but stayed in the embassy all night, catching a cat nap here and there, he finally managed to finagle an evening off to pay an uninvited visit to the party cell of the school board and raise holy Buddhist Hell about toxins in the classroom. Mom fastened her fingernails into his shoulder and tried to hold him back, pleading, "Father! Don't cause a scene! Don't shame us by making a nuisance of yourself! We're guests in this country, as I keep telling your brain-damaged daughter!"

Mom turned out to be right – not about brain damage, but about being a nuisance. Reprisal for the disturbance was immediate. Daddy's daughter was accosted the very next day by older kids from the upstairs grammar school, red-scarved

Young Pioneers and Junior Socialist Leaguers.

"Do your bones get any longer when the temperature rises in the summer?" they chortled around chronically swollen adenoids and tonsils. "You could use the extra height."

Of course, she had no idea what they were talking about. She was only able to interpret this treatment as bullying by squinting hard, and almost straight up, into their dazzling white faces, where she instinctively recognised broad sneers of sadistic glee.

They enticed her into the reading room and caused her to look at Chapter Three of their mimeographed Cyrillic primer, *Exploitation of the proletariat throughout the world*. The illustrations were pirated from an old *Look Magazine* exposé, and featured people who looked something like the scattered few Mongolian types in her class. Gifted Masako was already able to muddle through the few English captions that hadn't been cropped by the commissars, and they said the people in the pictures were actually Japanese. It followed that their faces must also have resembled her own, even though she'd lately been feeling quite white among all the vast Slavs.

Before being shown the *Look* photos, Masako had harbored only the vaguest suspicions as to why everybody, especially Comrade Svidrigailov, expected her to associate exclusively with the strange kids from out east. Barely able to speak, those eyeless outcastes were bussed, or rather trekked, in all the way from Irkutsk for ideological purposes, and to preserve correct appearances in this model school. They tended not to be the most exciting playmates in Eurasia, as they spent a lot of time gazing wistfully up into the sunless sky, tears streaming down their round faces.

But now it finally dawned on Masako that she'd been encouraged to find a desk among their unwashed ranks solely in consideration of the physical features she shared with them. With the strange objectivity of the very young, she began dispassionately to question the beauty that Daddy, if not Mommy, always claimed to see in her face.

Her Caucasoid classmates' gold, ivory and lapis-lazuli kissers were the very models for Likka-chan, the Shinjuku high-fashion doll. Masako and every other Japanese girl owned and loved Likka-chan, built whole inner worlds around her, and laid the foundations of their psyches on her escape-and-rescue adventures, co-starring similarly melanin-unencumbered plastic princes, sold separately. Once Masako had idly wondered aloud, within Mother's earshot, whether black-haired, almond-eyed dolls were manufactured anywhere in the world, and had gotten nothing but a blank stare, a silent pause, then a bemused chuckle, followed gently by, "Don't try to tell jokes. Humor is a difficult trick even for a male. You certainly haven't the intelligence for it."

The oriental faces in the *Look* exposé were among the few this tiny expatriate had ever seen depicted in something other than restaurant advertisements, and she examined them with interest, trying to learn about herself.

But all was not well with this particular bunch of Asians. They looked to be simple fishermen and their families, but were twisted and wadded like botched origami sculptures: limbs bent backward, eyeballs charlie-horsed, tongues lolled in square knots. Putting the best face on an unpleasant situation, as all good Nihonjin do, several of the less sorely afflicted in one photo tried to enjoy a hot bath together with their offspring. (The polar children hovering over Masako's shoulder giggled at least as much at the hairless nakedness as at the pain.) Through mimeographed steam, Masako's countrymen gazed with love into their sons' and daughters' unrecognizable, unrecognizing eyes.

In another picture she saw the administrative building of a nearby chemical plant, secure behind a living cordon of sumo-sized riot policemen. It was hard to believe that the blue-clad officers were born of the same stock as the withered and wasted freaks who swooned and waved protest signs among poison-vomiting culverts on the other side of the chain-link fence. And, though she didn't let on at the time, Masako was already able to read the Romanised name of her grandfather's corporation in the captions.

As if on cue, Comrade Svidrigailov chose that moment to stride into the lime-green reading room. At a glance she was able to see her proper course of action. The leaders deemed her unqualified to be placed in charge of the older pupils' nurture under normal circumstances; but this was a rare opportunity to exploit the special foreign student as a living, blushing object lesson.

"Have you looked into those people's eyes?" boomed Comrade Svidrigailov in her mannish voice. "The expression has been skewed not only by degeneration of the tissue underlying the eyelids, but by dissolution of the central nervous system. Their very senses were being perverted, therefore the universe itself was perverted, as far as they were able to ascertain. And their perceptions had just enough time to drive them insane with terror before the pure physical agony killed them. It would be very hard, my children, to imagine a more unpleasant way to leave this earth."

(A pause to wink broadly at the meanest sixth-grade boys, the sharp dressing sophisticates with well connected fathers, to whose French-wine-and-American-movie parties this social-climbing educator cherished faint hopes of being invited.)

"A certain young lady's family," continued Comrade Svidrigailov, "under the kind auspices of Japan's mighty Chisso Corporation, enriched those poor fish-workers' water with plenty of the runny silver which my kindergartners just studied. And, as you can see, it did not have the best effect on their general level of health, for they put it in their mouths, not just their hands. You didn't take a sip, did you, Comrade Masako?"

Titters were heard from a small mob gathering in the reading room. Comrade Svidrigailov possessed the emotional maturity of the least grown-up of them, but was better informed. So when she instigated the taunting, she was able to bring a more or less adult sting to it.

"Now I'm not saying there's any definite scientific connection. But the owners and operators of the offending plant, being rich enough to consume more than their fair share of the local catch, might develop a resistance to the disease. And you know there's a genetic component to class. Lenin said so. And capitalist exploiters do tend to produce a certain type of offspring..."

"Resistance?" snickered Anna Belov, whose little sister Masako had always fancied to be a borderline friend. "That must be why this Nip's face is only slightly lopsided, like the American WC Fields'."

"Yes," chimed in another behemoth kid. "She talks out of one side. A natural water carrier for a basketball team. She can pass on contraband instructions from the coach."

"Or she could be one of those interpreters that cower and mumble at the Jap emperor's elbow all day long."

"She's born for it."

"Interpreter, nothing. She acts like a princess herself."

"What about the slitty eyes? Did the thermometer juice cause that affliction?"

"They're all cursed with such eyes."

"The stuff must palsy the hands as well. That's why she's got such putrid handwriting."

"And, please don't forget, its atomic number is 200.59," Comrade Svidrigailov reminded everybody, deftly steering the discourse back onto the scientific track now that political obligations had been fulfilled.

Branded the justifiably tormentable spawn of black-class bourgeois reactionaries, Masako came home crying daily over the course of an entire semester. She was politely ignored until she started to disturb the downstairs neighbors' rest with screaming nightmares about her arms bending backward at the elbows and shattering like thermometers.

"Amend your ways," said Mom, finally, bedside, in a relatively soothing tone. It was deep night in their cavernous Moscow flat. Daddy was still at work, and Masako had just turned in a contemptible performance on the times-13 multiplication table. "You must work hard to learn what it is about yourself that provokes such discord among your co-evals," said Mom. "And correct it promptly before any more disharmony results from this weakness of yours, whatever it may be."

At that, the little girl's weeping got louder, and Mother continued her comments, unperturbed.

"There, there. I know it's hard to make yourself into a good citizen. But we must learn to put the best face on everything. Every experience has a silver sheen to it, if you've been born with enough basic intelligence to peer closely around the edges. We must fix on the good side. Your pain today will make you a better member of society tomorrow."

Mother shifted onto the other buttock and said, in a bedtime-story voice, "Once, when I was a stewardess, I allowed myself to be caught unawares by a pocket of clear-air turbulence and popped an upper vertebra on the cabin ceiling, starboard, aft. I was forced to remain supine for the remainder of the flight, not only depriving my fellow crew members of my help, but taking up precious space on the galley floor. And do you know what I did?"

Sleepy Masako didn't leap to reply, so Mom put the question again, more firmly – but first asking the child, rhetorically, of course, whether she'd been born with no eardrums as well as no penis and no cerebral cortex.

"What did you do?" asked Masako.

"Well, I'll tell you. The second I got out of the hospital – even though my co-workers were all foreigners and therefore congenitally incapable of forming even a rudimentary idea of what I was doing – I removed my shoes and kowtowed to them 10 times in the Air France stewardesses' central lounge, five-kilo neck brace and all."

"Was that in wonderful, beautiful Paris?"

"Not that it matters, but yes. Shall we review our Periodic Table of Elements now? What comes right after gold?"

"In our family?" asked Masako, and got a prompt good-night slap in return.

From that point on, the child began asking herself what good it would do to amend her ways when her sin was inherited, according not only to her teacher, but to the mean boys who got her alone in the stairwell and teased her in a dialect she comprehended only imperfectly.

"Your whole family," they said, "lives on the flesh of fishermen scooped dead from the silver sludge of Minamata Bay."

Little Masako began to weep into her pillow every night, more fiercely, in anger now as well as heartbreak. She only wanted to be friends with people, and the big kids were inciting even the token Uzbeks to shun her.

"That's just because they think you're an egghead," explained Dad one Sunday afternoon while she scrubbed his back. It was just the two of them awash in the white man-sized bathtub, an unprecedented treat, for her sisters were taking naps. He was speaking softly so his voice wouldn't bounce off the tile walls and into the kitchen. It would be better if Mom didn't hear him putting immodest sentiments inside her head.

"It's just because you can read two and a half languages already in kindergarten, and it's plain to see that you're going to learn more and more. Even your ridiculous teacher feels inadequate in front of you. That's the real reason everybody's so mean. The Minamata matter is just a smoke screen, a false charge trumped up by communists ashamed of their own mediocrity."

He looked up at the steamy light fixture, which might very well have been bugged, and added, in a much louder voice, "Petty envy is the crippling curse of the Marxist dispensation!"

But, a year later, back home in Nippon, "the Minamata matter" was exactly what a certain six-year-old would think she saw, caked and bursting from the hollows of a heat-split skeleton at a hillside crematorium. It was a special afternoon, when she was allowed to publicly display her dinner-table skills for the first time.

Masako had been pressed to early chopstick mastery by – who else? Mom believed, along with many of her compatriots, that such digital discipline, reinforced by its intimate connection with sustenance, somehow enhanced one's mathematical aptitude.

"Eating our rice with a pair of *hashi* from childhood on," explained Mom, "loosens up our built-in abacus. What do I mean by such a cryptic remark? Well, I'll tell you. We Nihonjin, in ancient times, perfected the secret art of using our fingers in calculating. Hence the discrepancy in math scores between our high school enrollees and the spoon-wielding barbarians on the far side of the Pacific. Here, fool, let me show you."

She grabbed Masako's hand and commenced dislocating digits.

"Thumb into the palm is one, followed by the index, two, and so on and so forth, until all four fingers have cloaked the thumb in an attitude unsuited for fist fighting."

(Later, as a student in Boston, Masako would learn that the number-five position was the male homosexual salute. It had seemed significant at the time, but she'd meanwhile forgotten how.)

In the event, Masako was able to hone these exquisite skills to the point where she was allowed to help her extended family pick through the few chunks of an unmarried old relative which had survived the consecrated incinerator – all according to the venerable traditions of her ancestral Buddhist sect.

Mother explained that, macabre as this ritual would seem to foreigners, the burnt bone-picking served a definite theological purpose in certain segments of Japanese society. It was a kind of inchoate Eucharist for closet ancestor-worshippers, a tip of the Buddhist hat to Nihonjin who might otherwise be disinclined to profess a foreign faith imported third-hand from the Asian mainland.

Masako's Daddy had given her a brand-new kid-sized black sequined clutch purse to go with the rest of her mourning outfit. To impress Mom with how well she was able to plan ahead and equip herself in advance, she had tucked into that purse her pretty new Hello Kitty chopsticks with the real moving eyes.

But Mom only wound up ridiculing her (in a whisper, of course) because, as anybody but a mongoloid cretin would know, crematoria provide their own chopsticks for the special task, cooking size, green and white ivory, to be left sticking upright among the beloved's remains in exactly the position which one was never, ever to leave one's regular hashi sticking in rice, because of the morbid (read unlucky) associations.

"I'm certain Great Auntie wouldn't appreciate being culled from this ash trough and placed into the memorial urn by cartoon character hashi," sneered Mom as they knelt with cousins and grannies around the sirloin-fragrant pit.

She paused to critically appraise her daughter's dishwashing job, then added, in a dour tone, "Especially not with a solidified grain of rice adhering to the left one. In any case, that chunk's too big to retrieve with chopsticks. Even if you were a sturdy boy and the pride of our household, you wouldn't have the finger muscles to do it. Nobody expects you to even try. It's foolish, as well as immodest and disruptive to the social order, for a dull girl like you to be such an overachiever. Content yourself with this wrist bone – and what's the New Latin term for it?"

In the vestibule of the Buddhist funeral parlor, Masako had watched her dutiful dad bop his fine mahogany-brown forehead on the floor at the feet of each wellwisher and condolence deliverer, including some uninvited ones: fishermen from the newly condemned bay – perfectly well-behaved, as their presence alone was disruption enough.

Shadow-lurking Minamata Grampa, having just lost a sister to more natural causes than they'd lost theirs, addressed a beautiful young monk in a whisper audible clear across the reception area, even over the roaring of the stoked furnace. He grumblingly described the unwashed intruders as "cheeky opportunists whose own genes can't produce worthy heirs, so they invent a scandal, cast aspersions on our pristine effluents, and try to tap the corporation for settlements – less euphemistically known as blood money – to finance them as they mop up after their deformed children. Well, they won't see a single aluminum yen from it! Not in my lifetime, by God!"

"I imagine not in theirs, either," murmured the monk as he surveyed the quaking, gasping interlopers.

At their twisted feet, meanwhile, Daddy kowtowed especially hard on the concrete, as if to drown out Grampy's unrepentant words, his skull sounding full of thickish fluid and about to burst like a shrunk-wrapped honeydew. And that was the first time Masako saw her loving Father's face crumple, his character, by all visible indications, sink into temporary but total disarray.

It was a measure of how little this sort of thing is talked about in polite Japanese society that she had to wait until she entered junior high school and enrolled in an AP biology course to find out that infection with the "Minamata matter" wasn't really hereditary at all. And even then she figured it out for herself, using an American textbook her father had brought home from the US Consulate library. Masako's biology teacher hadn't enough common scientific sense even to understand the question, and couldn't imagine why he should: nothing like it was scheduled to appear on any college entrance exams.

Speaking of such all-important examinations, already at the age of six Masako had been drilled by Mom in anatomy and several other morally unambiguous disciplines whose essences could be reduced to basic response conditioners, such as systems of flash cards. Nevertheless, with the enormous amounts of other information that had been compacted between the walls of her skull since that afternoon at the hillside ovens, Masako could not be sure that she'd correctly identified (had she identified it out loud?) a large, blackened, slightly greasy object as a femur.

Great Auntie's thigh bone – which, she hoped, smelled like an outhouse only in retrospect – had split wide open in the flames, and little Masako had seen, or thought she'd seen, oozing from where the barbecued marrow should've oozed, a certain liquescent substance, that terrible sauce, the curse of her clan.

The roasted marrow had seemed silvery, and she couldn't help thinking of the etymology of *sui-gin*. Her skeleton loaded with such gunk, Great Auntie would've indeed gotten taller, which is to say, better, worthier of love, had she survived into summer.

Earthenware more porous than metal, absorbs particles of the flesh

Kimberly Burwick

Epicurean – your swollen yellow skin. The morning I left you found
photographs, Seeing the Earth
from 80 Miles Up. German V-2 rockets in White Sands,
New Mexico.

October 1950. *National Geographic*'s faded pages
halved by nine AM glare
from the bay window where you are not fucking but holding
my photograph. Thin yellow hair ablaze
dust particles that had risen
long before the shutter
snapped.

Furniture that ruins wood when it is not carried but dragged
into the center of a unoccupied room. Grooves, coins,
pages stuck together from the evening I braised
quail.

One fifth of the time it took me to find sand
you crossed the living room, lit matches, launched fire on a colony of
ants.

In the criminal's cabinet, Holmes discovers himself

Jason Camlot

Holmes entered the cabinet
of the respectable reverend
(who was in fact a closet naturalist)
and found so many Victorian things.

There were teapots
and rare fatal cannons,
coffins filled with roses,
and tinted canvases in frames.

Along one wall were hats on parade,
and fabrics apparently
from the time of Moses.
Behind one glass case could be seen

brass of superior quality,
and effigies of a more primitive culture.
Behind another:
artistic applications of electrotype,

snuffed tapers and chandeliers,
and beneath a glass table top,
instruments for the manipulation of teeth.
Holmes admired the Japanned goods.

He wondered at the strange colonial livestock,
and the new technology in underclothes.
Umbrellas opened and closed mechanically.
Then he found the full collection of thimbles.

These tiny monstrosities of lead
he screwed onto his fingertips
to help explore himself further
without fear of poisoned needles.

Bring up a child in the way he should go

Sherry Chandler

Boys put playing cards in their spokes, eat
piles of buttered biscuits with blackberry jam.
They scorn dry toast, linens hand woven, crumbs
brushed neatly away. Boys wear the same
white shirt for days, read only comics and
the baseball scores. Oh I knew one was sent
to military school, learned to line
his socks up in neat rows. For he had read
Ginsberg and Jack Kerouac, slammed
the heavy church door in the Father's face.
He wants discipline the voices cried.
We cannot leave him in this error. He
must learn the ways of boys who will be boys.

[the return of the ring]

Maxine Chernoff

a fault-based
approach
ends in a break-up
(of rituals
and rites,
      their permutations)
did, for instance,
the parties
      have
      a hasty proposal
nothing
in common
         hated in-laws
a hostile child
disagreeable pets
          untidy habits
      a view of what
      went wrong
         in the promise
      makes us believe
         in fairness & truth
(though Roman law
says
      he gets
the ring – she
      a penalty
for reneging)
the rule of life
      as rule of law
you break
it off
      you lose
the gift
unless she's
at fault
      (and leaving town)

which might mean
trickery
      and cover
  of night
(I picture Mae West
or a film
noir blonde
with sultry eyes
      and a cash
register mind)
       "give back the ring
get on with your life"
      is common sense
(minus
insult & rage)
both parties
      walk
away
from the scene
      like dancers
who slump
            after the dance
yet
we hope
to learn
from things
      a lesson
transmuting
gold
      into grace

Farmy

Todd Colby

We followed a line of fragrant flowers
that plagued the roadside with splashes of vexing color.
At the rest stop you stood next to the road with a sign
that instructed the motorists to veer away
from the green cordage, and dirt shoulder.
Suspiciously heavy dark raindrops pummeled our skulls
and reminded us to bring our heads back in the window
in order to have a glance around inside the car now and then.
It didn't take us long to discover that our foreheads
were mottled with specks of blood, and the thuds against our heads
were actually shiny black bugs, with tiny, razor-sharp legs.
There's still so much bleak, backbreaking work to do in the heather;
I don't know if we'll ever get it done.
The fields are greasy; even the breezes are greasy.
I never was one to fight in a car,
especially if someone wanted to fight
to get out of the car while the car was still moving.
Quite frankly, that has never been on my agenda.
Pieces of hair blow by in the breeze:
some of it red, some of it blond and shimmering;
it's the visual equivalent of a stern reprimand.
I don't know where you are, but I'm getting there.

The fitness of the human heart

MTC Cronin

Our hearts are shrinking to fit our chests. From our hands grow the shadows of wolves but the little dog of our face is cowardice. We wanted the war. When the first death passed like a small cloud we did not seek its reflection in the stream but drank there with our sons and daughters. Across our breasts we held our shadows. We all put different things in front of our hearts. We rolled a stone. Do you see what we see? The idea of the cave that would not be left.

The internal life of a brick

Kieran D'Angelo

It was thick in there, every movement pressed something else, demanded movement. I felt myself held on all sides. Sounds juddered through me, solid ripples tiding the stone. It was all stone, and its bitter dust stuck my breath. Every move for life made certain my killing as the stone inched into me. Muscle, my lungs, liver, wetflesh, were part of the stone. All one, and sure I would keep pushing, working, as long as I could, within the stone, resisting the stone, part of the stone... and then it would meet itself again. It would crush me, work me without malice, the *knowing* in the stone. I. Bloodwrung, stonejoined, iron in stone, zinc in stone... my share of the stone. All one and through with stone.

Cracks came in my sleep, enough to be aware of my head hurting, the nightmares sourced in the pains and the pains a means to their ends. The net curtains billowed and I could hear the traffic outside. I was wet. The air seemed to be thick with water, as if it were weeping, soaked with cloud and dripping over me, over my bed. I shook awake and realised I was really wet, the bed was wet. I leaped free, stood naked and wet till my brain furnished the necessary causal chain. I was like a three-year-old learning to count, dumbhorse nodding with each number in the chain – water/water falls/water falling/falls from up/look up... on the ceiling was a great dark blemish about the light rosette... The Squatters, the filthyarsed lowdown miscreant smackhead squatters.

I hauled the mattress clear, popped a bucket below the drip. I dragged clothes over my wet skin and raced up the stone stairs to the third and final floor. Knocks on the door to no response, no movement.

I balled my fist and banged on it, four-five. No nothing. Anything could be happening/not happening. Could be dead, could be gone. Prank or punishment for a slight, an imagined one cause I've never done anything but try to ignore them.

There was a load of stuff on the landing. Stolen bicycles chained to the rail, stocks of twisted and useless metals, cooker parts, prams, broken glass, soft refuse and ancient phone books, one of which I took up for smacks at the door. The softened spine bashed at the shivering wood, wrestling the frame. Shockshakes ripple, downround the coldaired stairwell, like plugsucked water.

"First time in two years you come up them stairs and you're knockin' at *their* door!"

I don't look, cause it's Angela, and it's normal for us to pretend that the other's not there. It's like a little dance with known steps, but one which never goes past the bows and feints.

"I don't know! What are you like!" says her voice which skips when she wants it to, whips when she wants it to, always sings clear of the meaning, the tawdriness of the things we find the space to say. It's a voice far wiser than the words she's learned.

She was wearing dark blue jeans, which *fit* but don't hug, with immense, fluffy pink slippers below and a short sweat shirt, pink too – it showed her long, level collarbones, and hung just below her waist line. As she moves it swings, just a little, from her tonetight midriff. She's not so narrow in the waist, nor the hip, nor the shoulder. She looks amazing in a swimsuit, one-piece.

Feet forward at the end of the slope of her legs, feeling the stretch in her calves, she tally reclines against the door of her mum's apartment where she's lived all of her 24 years.

I keep bashing at the door, thinking about my flat flooding, thinking I want to cripple the greasy indolent fools who live inside. Or don't. At the start of the summer, one of their happy-go-lucky crew OD'd. Went all the way from here to over the hill in a flatlaid spazzy choke on the floor. It's like drowning, dying that way, the wild eyes, the violence, then the slow, still swoop to the peace of sands. So... this bird's crew watched her twitch and flail, and then not – and they all moved out. They called the ambulance people who came for the corpse, and after a grace period of some hours, they moved back in, baby, bikes, lifted hardware, broken glass, smack-plated spoons, needle litter, pizza boxes and all manner of rat incubating filth. So it was the usual – music all night, morgue peace in the day, coming and going all night. Concrete chink on the stairs, voices echo, lugging the stolen bikes, lugging em out and sold. People coming and going, buying smack, sometimes cash, some barter... objects/people/slamming/cars/rows/ stamping quivers my ceiling, quivers the air comes to my ear/my eyes/nose/touching me, ripples/waves/tides in the internal life of a brick.

"Well, if you won't tell me what's going on, I can't help you!"

She even sounds a little annoyed. However it's pitched, there's something about that voice that reaches me. A scientist, sadly, might say, it's the right frequency to shiver something inside me, some primal urge or something. I just think I like it, like it, yes I do. I hate to hear her speak to another man that way, though I've no right to feel that way except the sound itself is cause.

Another voice, "Angela! What are you doing there? There's a draught."

"It's him downstairs, Mum, The Lord of the Manor. He's got some sort of *problem*. Throwing a wobbly all over next door."

Naomi came into the hall, suddenly full of her, all of us suddenly full of her. You could tell, by the precise width at which her feet were planted in their conservative heels that she was in charge. She wore an ivory blouse and a sleek black skirt; yellow washing-up gloves too, lit with popping suds. Her head was a little cocked back which emphasised the smooth sweep of her belly, up to her full bosom.

She looked over her glasses. Her hair pulled back tight, it emphasised her smooth forehead; the line flowed to a caucasian atavism in the nose, but there's something Bedouin, something adamant and decided in the bone, a holy clarity of sand, sky, fire and water. Her skin is the colour of dates.

"Don't lean up like that, Angela. Like you waiting for something."

Angela ignored her. "What's going on?" Angela asked me.

"They're flooding my flat. Water pouring through the ceiling."

Angela's lips purse a fleshy burst and flatten out.

"Are they there? Did you hear them go out?" I say, still hammering.

"I haven..."

"*She* in there," said Naomi, making a face. "He went out to make mischief. I saw him scuttle like a rat. Some *errand* he running for her." Naomi always sounded with high precision, sounds brought forth from a high and eclectic library, floating unmauled through a measured diaphragm. She selected from a great range of tone, accent, syntaxes and vocabulary, but she had always been unwavering in value, sometimes rigid. No more than 43/4 and handsomer than many women half her age, she's in danger of becoming brittle, like a slowly freezing waterfall once diamond with tantalising frost.

I didn't like what I was hearing, on any level. If *she*'d come to the door at all, you couldn't say what would happen. I'd see *him* now/again, shuffling about, bearded, by negligence rather than design, and he kept his eyes down from me.

I've got my eye to the wrongside of the spyhole until I see light cut.

Then nothing.

"Look," I say, leveltoned. "You're flooding my flat. I just need you to stop flooding my flat. That's all."

My guess was she wouldn't want to push me too far, but you couldn't tell with someone so disarranged. In as much as the flat's occupants had a yardstick of reality, of what they could get away with, she was it. She was the instrument of insertion, the thin end of their wedge. She'd washed up here, alone, about a year ago clinging to a suitcase and a pram. She was paying rent then. It was a new start, she said, after the break-up; "life-lessons," she said. "You can't love someone who doesn't want to be loved", she volunteered after about four minutes' acquaintance. She shook her head, looking at me from between the gingerish strands that fell to either side of her eyes, then let them shade her face.

I helped her in, in fact. She was struggling with the main door, first day, the knack of the lock and I opened it for her, helped with the shopping etcetera. As I stooped to pick up the bags I heard the sight of her feet walk quickly by. Gratitude was lavish, at least in smiles. She seemed to take it all very personally. I was, she could tell, a man who respected motherhood, and she made much play of the pram, driving it at me, encouraging me to chook and coo at the pallid sprog. I'm not saying she planned all that happened, but does a seed plan to grow? She borrowed, she liked to borrow sugar, eggs, tea, vacuum cleaners. She begged lifts, lifting, waiting in, waiting for, waiting till, all in the name of the child. Every contact left something done, some *touch*, established a precedent, a flow of energy, from you to her. A little while later, Aubrey-downstairs found that a credit card had been issued in his name and run to four grand over a period of a week. Soon afterward she got a car. She would park it in the space that custom, in a place where custom had withered, still accorded to Naomi. Of all the people in the building, she seemed most intent on hurting Naomi. Though perhaps Naomi was merely closest. Then, the boyfriend arrived, and it began in earnest. It wasn't a campaign, more like a *persuasion* of symphonic complexity. The silences between the noises were even more eloquent than the eruptions of music and thumping, the dragging and humping, wailing and a-moaning. It was these that let you know the value of peace in between the notes *and* who owned it. It was like something growing on your skin. It was an experiment in degradation, like slowly mixing pus into a baby's feed, spooning it to him, not killing the baby but letting it grow with the poison, then rubbing his stunt, tweaking the stunt to keep it raw, excited... Ki-ki-come on liddle bebee, ead a liddle more. Yes-you-can-yes-you-can, do it for mama... like heroin, getting used to heroin, accommodating heroin, as she was, as we all were. We accepted it, in exchange for intact windows, no shit through the letter box, not being a target for a break-in by one of her comers and goers. In a way, she could say, I was under her protection. "Don't you worry about it," she said, showing her rotted teeth, "Don't you worry about it," she said, showing a largesse of rotten teeth when I expressed reservations about the shifting cast of people running up and down the stairs, the number of keys apparently extant to the communal front door. "But it must be a worry, living alone," she said – she'd been alone too, she knew what it was like. Her greatest weapon is the unreason we all sense lurks at the root of her, the self-hatred which will allow her to tear at her own life to upset ours. She's got us all over a barrel cause she's holding herself hostage! Genius.

But there's something she doesn't know. Of the six flats accessed by this stairwell, two on each floor, one to either side of the stair, I own three; the one where I live and the one below Naomi's, where some Moroccans live and the one below that, where Naomi's sister, Diana, lives with her husband, Aubrey, mild Aubrey.

She's underestimated my interest. I want her out, the needle-whore, her baby, her boyfriend. Today.

I heard bolts give on the other side.

"Be careful," Naomi said. "He doesn't have enough in him to make this," she gestured to the foul mess that squatted outside her flat, "His are the hands, but the wickedness is hers," she pronounced. She was something of a bibliac.

She pulled Angela inside and quietly shut the door.

All you have to do is delve into my brick and you'll find her. Pick her up, pinched and wriggling, but careful case she bites. A splendid specimen of a skinnyshanked shabbytitted needle-whore.

There's just a face over the security chains, T-shirt over knickers, and some leg. She's showing leg! And using. Bleary eyes. Grey like dying skies.

But she just looks at me. Nothing ventured/nothing asked for.

I talk slowly. She's a long way from here and has to be dealt with gently. Don't trample on her shame. The sight of Naomi tramples on her shame. I speak as if she is an animal, that can only comprehend tone, not the words themselves. "I think you've left your bathroom taps on. There's lots of water pouring through my ceiling, into my bedroom."

"Oh," she says, the thoughts moving slowly through, jaw loose, "I'll..."

"Yes."

She feels her face, beneath her hanging hair, "I want..."

"Yes."

She perks up a bit, her head lifts. "It's a good job you came," she says, "I was going to be late for an appointment. Overslept."

"Ah," I say, "It's an ill wind... but you've found the silver lining!"

"Right," she says, as if I've detained her long enough.

"Don't forget," I say winningly.

"I won't," she says heartily, "Don't worry."

"Great," I say, "Thanks."

As the one door closed another opened.

Angela... "Do you want to come in for tea?"

"Whose idea's that?"

She smiled, opened the door wide so I had to walk by her. I wandered in to their home's assault in colour. Everywhere colours were combined/laid/fought with one another, like cockerels in a farmyard. Everywhere was an event in colour, in glass birds, in fabric Jamaicas, in Ghanaian headscarves, like teeming flowers, all vying for the light in the eyes, grouped round huge photos of loved ones. Faces twice large to life-sized, or football teams of relatives, in Jamaica, Trinidad, Ghana, the US, brought together for a week to celebrate their blood, to catalogue their similarity, wonder at their difference. A different readiness to see blooms for a while within me, then a faint dismay that it's all too much for me, eyes weaned on greyskies and near horizons, curtailed affections.

By custom, Angela and I seat ourselves in the living room where Naomi will bring tea. Angela throws herself into the armchair, legs shot over the arm. She doesn't look and waits for me to speak. Generally, I've done the talking, the deciding and she has followed, over fences, through the parks... The first time I stole a car, a Citroën 2CV, I picked her up at school.

"What did she say, Miss Poison Drawers?"

"Said she was sorry. But I did put my flat under hers. And I really should have thought about that before I did it."

"You've only yourself to blame."

"Yeah," I said wearily. "Just being me at the wrong time with the wrong face."

"What I can't believe is that she's got a baby. And this is the life she's made around it! This was a good building before she came, clean, quiet, nice people," she said making a little sardonic movement of the head toward me. "If I had a baby, I'd think about everything I did and said. Whether it was good for my child. I'd make a world around it, little by little, like watering the garden. Plan everything around it. That's what mothers do."

"Well, she certainly makes plans. She's a black hole of plans and we're all being sucked into it."

I sat in the chair built into the sewing machine. I wanted to fix on something that was not moving. I tapped on the heavy cast tabletop, eyeing the feminine waisting of the machine, feeling the shaped marsupial seat beneath my buttocks. I mushed into it, feeling the radiator at my back. A generation of children in the district had worn clothes from that machine and until recently the young mothers had still dragged the tots up the stairs to be measured for Naomi's tailored attentions. She could look from her window and see them all walking up and down. The mothers knew to be grateful even though they'd paid. It was like a club. When the needle-whore had arrived, Naomi gave the sprog an anorak.

That sceptic bitch, I muttered to myself.

I've no wish to break the quiet which is a familiar one, and my eyes click over the spines of the wall-to-wall records, Angela's dad's records, and other nostalgia. He had a huge record collection, blues and reggae mostly, but it was catholic of the white British bands of the Sixties, Cream, The Yardbirds... he liked The Stones particularly, *Exile on Main Street* especially. He had not a shred of use for The Doors.

It was what he did, bought and sold records – buying round the Caribbean, the eastern seaboard of the US, selling out of a shop in Ladbroke Grove, a stall on Portobello. "Real black music! For real black people!" He wore American clothes, he'd bluffed an American passport, but he loved cricket; he always said that one day/ some day he and I would go to a game of baseball... "When you've seen baseball, then you'll appreciate what an E-vent is a day's cricket!"

Angela more resembles her father than Naomi. She's lighter-skinned than her mother. It's skin shot with found gold from the oceans' bed, where it eases and laps between the islands of her parents' birth. She's rounder faced and the skin is taut and liable to adventures in emotion. Eyes have an Asiatic depth, a trueblack glint, but her eyelids are spacious, lashes luxurious. A feral crease can take her smooth nose into a scowl though no mark remains when it passes... and now she's ready, hiding a smile, as I/we, our eyes chime...

"Where is he?" I asked. "What's he up to?"

"Florida. He's got a house in Florida; nice house, with a swimming pool, a couple of German Shepherds.

"Eh?"

"And a girlfriend."

A grin welled from inside till my face was taken with it. I was in no mood to smile but I had no choice. Mac.

"She's only thirty," she snickered.

I clenched a vigorous fist for my man, Mac.

"He says he can cope!" she said.

"Yah! He'll be fine," I said.

"You say! This a proper blackwoman we're talking about!"

"..."

"Anyway, he's sending me some money. I'm going to go in the winter. Get away from..."

"How long for?"

"Don't know," she watched me, and then stopped. I looked at her hands, as did she, looking at me looking at... She had long fingers, curving thumbs. "Don't like America that much. But I'm not doing that much here. Am I?"

"Should go," I said.

"I am."

"No. *I* should go. See the baseball."

"Yeah! He always said he'd take *you* to a game."

Angela and I, we're just looking at each other.

Angela sat up, dressing herself in sudden discovery – eyes wide/a little gasp – but it's a mismanaged outfit, more as if coffee spilled in her lap.

"Sometimes I think you miss Dad more than I do."

"Nah. Don't be silly."

"He didn't take much interest in me."

I was scandalised. It violated some sacred tenet, some Macology I kept like a family snap.

"Oh, No! It wasn't that he didn't... doesn't love me. He just wasn't interested in me. He didn't know where to start. He just thought I was a doll to dress up." She waited. "A girl to spend money on."

"No."

"Yes. But my mother didn't make it any easier."

She laughed.

I shook my head and nodded at the same time.

"I said that to her, that you missed him more than me... D'you know what she said? That when *you* miss him, you feel sorrier for yourself than I do. That was the difference."

"!!!!"

Angela nodded and shook her head all at the same time.

"Is that what you think?"

"No," she said. "If you do, which I don't really think you do, it's because of other things."

There was the surprise of his width, looking up as a child, up those long legs, and the arms which came down almost to his knees, but which stopped, just in time. I'd usually see him walking, a walk cast in the islands and tempered in American cities. It was short gaited on his high legs, legs like that he should have been gangly but he wasn't – he was suddenly deep-chested and wide in the shoulder, huge-handed... Spacious, he was spacious. His body tilted forward slightly from his narrow hips, but it didn't move when he walked, cept a little little swing in the shoulders from which his long long raincoats flowed. He wore them open and flowing in the wind, belt trailed, buckle swung toward the earth far below his head. Angela and I walked in the lee of that raincoat. You could tug on the buckle if you had a problem and you could get all the way down Ladbroke Grove without ever having to change direction, as long as you stayed in its shade. His name was Philip MacDonald but everyone called him Mac, and they liked to do it, liked to say his name... "Mac! Hey, Mac!," "How are you, Mac?!" and in his easy rumble, with a comfortable and fearless amiability, he'd trot out some disarming and agreeable rubbish, made in America, like "What time it is, my man, what a time it is!!" Across broad American streets, I see him calling something equivalently English or Jamaican to those demanding their MacMoment – *What you see is what you want* – I love people like that. In London, he drove an old red Mercedes tricked with white trim. And then he didn't, cause one time he went to America and didn't come back, or if he did, he favoured other portions of these isles...

Angela cocked her head, listening. "She's going out, her-over-there."

We were habitual conspirators... "Find out where she's going," ...so she didn't ask why and went out on to the hall.

"She's going to the dole office and then the supermarket."

"How long will it take?"

"Forever, if you believe her. 'It's all too much...,'" Angela wailed, "'the queues, the forms...'"

"Yeah, she's gonna suffer," I said as I left the room.

I went to my flat, grabbed my cellphone, some work gloves, other bits and pieces that make things in the world easier to change.

Watching the water fall, I called a locksmith, one of the guys I used to maintain my properties, Xavi's people.

"Half an hour. Need you here in half an hour."

"Can't do it, Guv. Snowed under."

"There's thirty over your rate."

Silence. Conference beyond.

"Foughty."

"40."

"See you when, Boss, see you then."

As I left the flat, I looked in the hall mirror and I saw Mac looking over my fifteen-year-old shoulder into the very same mirror as I inspected my fifteen-year-old face before we went out, Mac, Angela & Me.

"You're just not used to the sight of yourself yet," he said. "Going to be ok. Just got to wear your face in a little."

That was the last thing of significance he said to me. After that, the rest was just Machismo, anytime anyplace anyone.

I can't breath for memories in this place. Like a crushgilled fish in dead waters.

I went back up toward Naomi's flat.

Foot on the final stair, I hear ...

"He don't *fix* nothing, girl! He decided to stop fighting with himself and start to fight with other people. That's all."

"You think you have an easier time with him because he's *white*?"

A door slams.

I had a hammer in my hand and I brought it on the links that held the bicycles. The door opened, and I'm under Naomi's haughty gaze. She peers over her glasses at me...

My first thoughts about sex were triggered by Naomi, by sight of her in cotton dresses in summertime. The way the cloth gathered in the slope between her thighs as she sat in my grandmother's kitchen, unconscious of the small boy's big eyes, the wordless thoughts... or perhaps sharing glances about it with my grandmother on a frequency I could not yet detect. Time's made her deeper in the belly, richer in the bosom, but I think she's given up on sex. What she does with the energy that surely resides in her good good body, I don't know. Maybe she feeds it to a growing calm inside her, enjoying her power over it and savouring its diminution. She watches it ebb away, like some dangerous and ugly animal kept in a cage in a corner of her room. Thinking... she must not weaken, must not feed it... then and only then can it be delivered from the shaggy misery of its hunger.

I'm only speculating. I think rather that her game's too high for me and I can't approach it. She looks at me as if I'm fragile, up and down, through and through a thin thing. It makes no difference how much I puff and expand. "Not fighting with yourself," she says, "is everything." She gives me little lectures on her method of being, *keeping an intact heart*, she calls it. She attends church but no longer with Angela, and has a good job with the council, an education officer. She affects glasses; I tried them on once, for Angela's amusement, trying to take her mother off. My vision is A1. And so's Naomi's. There is no medicine in those lens! They're air and light frozen to glass, like a filter between her and the world, just a little *process* before it gets to her. She always peers over them, watching TV from across the room, driving, reading, even when her hands spread and coax the cloth below the drive needle of the sewing machine. I always stared, always amazed at the colour difference between her palms and the backs of her hands, the flesh itself, the adept flesh rhyming the long bones.

"Do you have any detergent?" I say.

"What for?" Angela says from behind Naomi. Naomi's not removed her hand from the door. Her rare eyes are rounded, lighter than her skin and liquid...

"To deter them," I say. "I'm gonna turn the place over while they're out. Change the locks. All of it. They're gone."

Naomi's eyes ask, over the glasses. They're a wall and a quizzical space where she can play with you, between the eye and the lens: you see *you* under the lens. You hear your voice in the silence there, and you speak to fill it... you try to say what you think she wants to hear. If you don't you fall fall fall through her silence, with your own voice sounding in your ears...

"There'll be keys for everyone but her. I'll settle with her landlord. I'll take full responsibility."

"Right?"

"Right."

"OK. You ask me for nothing, Right?"

"Right."

"And that's what I give to you. Right?"

"Yeah, Naomi, sure. Nothing happened. We're not having this conversation."

"Okay." She favours me with a little nod. "How will you get in? That door's too strong for your kicks."

"Bathroom window above mine, they always leave it open. There's a good drain-pipe. They don't make em like that anymore."

"Be careful."

My turn for silence.

You treat me like a stranger. Worse than.

The sight of me beaches on those rare eyes. She's been like this since I moved back in, when my grandmother died.

Angela comes, clutching bottles of virulent antibiotic cleansers, sprays, scalding powders.

"Leave 'em there," I say, "I'll be back for them. Out of *her* door!" and I make off down the stairs.

"Where are you going, Angela?" I hear. "This doesn't need you."

"He does. Someone's got to be there if he falls."

We went down to my flat.

"First time in a long time I've been in here."

"Without a chaperone."

We took a look at the flood, Angela just peeking round the bedroom door.

"Don't go in for much comfort, do you."

"You could leave them slippers down here," I said.

"..."

"Hoo! Does she have it in for me!" I said.

"She's just rubbish. She doesn't care about you one way or the other."

"Who?! No. Not her. Your mum."

She looked at me.

"No. You're wrong about that."

I walked away, opened the bathroom window. Cold air rushed in and we poked our noses out, elbowing for space. The traffic roared round the roundabout, round and round, like a choked sink trying to evacuate.

"Give me your phone," she said.

"Nothing's going to happen."

She held her hand out.

In the red Mercedes we would go to the cinema, Mac, Angela and I. She was always very well dressed – they favoured red on white for her, or white on red, or pink on white, pink ribbons. Lovingly stitched into the world by Naomi, little fur trimmed hoods hid her head from the cold, and her little face peeked out, rarely sighted. Sometimes she carried a little bicycle bell and would creep up behind people and ring it, sky-highing the clucking widows at the bus stops. In the Merc, Mr Mac would always seat me in the front, expressly, and we would visit the big American cartoons, Disney, of course, and he would fill his pockets with chocolate and crisps. To Angela, he would feed them in a teasing game until she waved them away, *Candy Girl*, he called her, while to me he would pass them side-on without taking his eyes off the film, like they were cigarettes. I'd would eat them quickly with an agreeable sense of contraband. Hotdogs were limitless on these forays in Americana. Sometimes he would say, *look at this!/you got to see this!* at some splendid effect and we would look at him, and the shapes reeling on his dark eyes. I realise now he had seen them before and I conjecture that it was with other children in some other place, perhaps far enough away that the seasons were different. Something in me prefers not, for Angela's sake, for Naomi's, but somehow I love it so... I hope he had more than one child for he was a handsome man all through, a genetic aristocrat. His presence put heat in those less full souls around him. He fed their belief in life. Not order, or wealth, but *life*, essential vitality, but one rested on a wholesomeness inviolable by circumstance or misfortune, not on virulence, dirty tricks. He prospered, Philip MacDonald. His was a life of luxury; everywhere he sat or stood or ate, he was inside himself.

As Angela watched, I stuck my head out of the window of my window and checked the squatters' window. I appraised the joints that rivetted the pipe to the wall. It was old enough to be made to last, but not yet old enough to have decayed. I shook it. Good, still.

"Bring me my shoes upstairs, yeah?" and I stuffed my socks into them.

"Be careful."

I put my feet on the ledge, and compacting myself, getting every fibre as close to the next as it would go, I put hands and feet onto the pipe at the same time, swung free, keeping bands of pressure allthrough, my body clamping like a fitting on the pipe. I smile at Angela and her lips twitch, her nose fidgets. She's not convinced. Not much use to me. The traffic sounds loud. Not far, but it was a big effort, a lot of pressure on my heart. Like doing a palm tree but without the organic hug. Looking down at Angela, tight-faced, looking at me looking at her, I fiddled awkwardly with the window catches, and I was inside, into the predictably noxious bathroom.

I kept quiet, listening. My one worry was for some soggy useless-piece-of-shit to be lying about sleeping-it-off under a pile of rancid blankets.

I crept through, looking, ferrethead round doors... relief ran through me, I stood straight, losing the skinky creep. Letting my feet come down hard, I marched into my new demesne, the conqueror. I went to the front door and opened it wide, to let the air in, my hordes pile through.

I opened the windows in the front, opening, opened. I felt free, proud and angry. Irresistible. I took a semi-sized TV from among the several. I threw it out of the window. It plummeted to the pavement two floors below, past my own window.

Breathing hard and excited, I looked out and over, over the facing building, and wondered at what a difference fifteen feet up can make, the jilt in perspective. I could see the horizon beyond. In all the years I'd been in this brick I'd never seen the horizon from the window. All that my own windows had presented was the flat trap of the blank face of the brick beyond. It had been my horizon, the same building echoed on my eyes, as precisely similar as my own face in the mirror.

Mac had prognosticated wonderful futures for me – "That's what I like! This boy's a noisy boy. He'll make some noise in the world. He's like that...whatsisname..." It was Mac's conceit, I think now, to pretend he didn't know things he did and had to work to recall them, like most others – "That tennis player always shouts and screams till he gets his way."

"It's disgraceful," said Naomi, about the tennis player, I think, "What kind of an example does that set? Philip?"

I remember how her lips folded and touched together when they formed *philip*.

"But he wins. Time come, end of the day and he walks away with the trophy, and the money. In 20 years time, everyone will have forgotten all that, and he'll be all mellow and cool with everyone. They'll only be thinking how much they enjoyed seeing him play and shout and scream at the stiff-assed umpire on his big baby chair. He cussed him out good! *You are the pits of the earth! You can not be serious! Heh-heh. Heh-heh-heh...You can not be serious.*" And on inspiration, Mr MacDonald dangled me out of the window, but no-one worried he'd drop me. "They'll just remember how good he was and how young they were when he was young." And he looked at Naomi, as he brought me back to earth, and she turned away.

"I'm a God-fearing man," he said.

"Why should you fear God?" she said. "I don't fear God. Why should anyone fear God?"

"That would all be fine, Naomi, really.... if you didn't fear Life instead."

She said nothing.

"You've got no imagination," he said. "Things..."

She did not draw breath. She did not hesitate...

"*You* have no imagination. You can't see where your steps are taking you. As surely as the night follows day, they will take you. That things follow a course in this world, just as the river runs to the sea, as the sea meets the sky on the horizon. Of a certainty. There are certainties written into this world. Maps where the wise set their feet. Can you not see the horizon? Philip? And when you cannot see it, do you not know it's there? If you call wisdom a lack of imagination then I will settle for a lack of imagination any day, every day... and live with the consequences."

It was an end of things, though he would visit for another ten years, and nominally be her husband. Angela near to grown, he stopped coming. What was he doing, I wonder now? Something tucked in among his reggae discs?

Words of that weight wing their way across time and fix on other tongues.

That was in my grandmother's living room, the room below this one. Angela was standing behind us and silent. Angela has always been instinctually silent. Apart from the bell, she moves softly and without warning, seeming to anticipate the play, so she's hanging around, waiting for it to come to her. And now Angela's standing beside me, 13 feet above where she was standing then, listening to the giants throwing boulders over the valley. She's wearing pink slippers on her feet instead of a pink ribbon in her hair, and I climbed in the window instead of being dangled out of it. Mr Mac's disappeared over the horizon, and her mother wears glasses with no real lens in them. Everything else is upside down and back to front... just like it should be, and always was, and always will be. For a few years, when we had actually been born yesterday, we didn't know...

"Yo! Monkey-Bwoayy!" she says in full Jamaican. Her eyes follow mine mine to the crashed TV. "Ooo. Ooo. His Lordship's in a right strop. We'd all better stay out of his way," she said, staying close.

"*Droit de seigneur,*" I mutter.

"What's that?"

"Nothing worth repeating."

"That's what you say when you've said something rude."

I put on my shoes. I begin to throw detergent over the beds, on the carpet. I take out my mallet and Angela pads away, short steps, her head very still...

... And she comes back with a pair of tailoring shears in gloved hands. Bending at the waist, with a cutlass flourish, she puts the blades to the fabric on the mattresses, plunges splits into the stuffing with the furrowing blades. Then she takes up the detergent and does again what I had done, does it for keeps.

I admire her buttocks, her thighs' long, effortless kiss.

My hands lay on her waist, feel of cotton, flesh beneath. She turns quickly, surprised, smiling but scissors high. A couple of playful snips in the air and she drops them, not caring where. Her lips are warmer than I've known...

She turns quickly, looking at me/looking at her... she gets about something else...

I pull the towels and toiletries onto the floor. Douse them. I stamp on powders, kick them around, slash the shower curtain, snap the rail from the wall.

She pulls a small ballpeen from the back of her jeans. On the draining board, in the sink, she aims the ballpeen, to tap tap tap her way through the crockery. A pile of fragments grows.

I mallet the mirrors, the bathroom cabinets. I smash the pipes below the sink with a Bruce Lee knee-breaker and tear down the curtains, douse them. For no good reason, I tear a phone directory in half, soak the pages in some antibiotic cleaner, throw them round.

She laughed.

"Not bad."

I smile, like, *Check me!*

"My dad could do *two!*"

"Yeah, well, I'm sorry I'm not your dad."

"Oh!" she exclaimed and her face creased, the eyebrow curling up the smooth forehead. The first telltale of a line..."Oh! It was terrible! Whenever he had a glass of rum with someone who'd never seen him do the show, he'd start tearing up the phone books! We never had *Yellow pages* till I was fifteen!"

I dragged the fridge from the sidewall and faced it on the floor for execution. The contents spewed out the open door. Gut it from the back.

"Is there anything you want?" she asked, "Any of the electrics?"

"What?"

"The gadgets."

"What? You gonna nick em?!!"

"What do you take me for?!! A *tief*, like you? You da tief round here!"

Like her mum and dad, she was picky about vocabulary, accent.

"Nah. I don't want nothing they got. 'Cept what's mine that they got. Like my peace of mind."

She presses her lips... she's silent a moment and decides to say something she's been wanting to say...

"That's not you. I like you better when you talk posh."

Then she goes to the appliances, the stereo, the fridge, the intricacy of wires behind the washing machine, the kettle, the TVs – she snips the cables, the aerial before the box, after the box, and finally, she goes to the mains box, and the *coup de grâce*; she flips the cordon of fuses, one by one, the finger stroking them off, pop pop. She looks at me, looks back to the box,...

"Should I do this?" she says.

"Yeah. I'll tell the landlord they did it. Let fucking Ajay pay. It's gotta cost him something, our suffering. Fucking lawyers and court orders! What a cunt!"

...and with a tipsnip of the scissors, she finally violated the power supply.

She jumped up, spins in the air.

"Yes!" she shouts, "Yes!"

She looks at me looking at her, her head cocks a little to one side – Looking at me?! Looking at me looking at you?

"Terminate. With maximum prejudice," my larynx set to CIA.

"I *hate* them. I hate what it does to my mum. I didn't want them to even have one-thought about staying. This is not a *challenge!*"

She goes away and comes back with a box – she takes the baby's bottle steriliser and she puts it in the box and she takes it over to her flat. When she comes back she nods/I nod, through the solid featured, impassive face we both wear for our silent work, but I'm breathing hard and she's not.

"I'll tell her some men came," she says.

Yeah," I say, "Black guys/white guys/brown guys, no-kind of guys – coalition of the willing."

"I'll bring her up to have a look. I'll tell her I saved this. For the baby."

"She'll love you for it."

"She'll think I love her, she's so mad!"

"She'll probably try and move in with you."

"As long as she don't run into the landlord..."

"No-one's gonna know nothing."

"An' even if someone guesses, which Ajay will, no-one's going to do nothing. Not worth it. Move on."

"She don't wanna see the landlord."

"She don't wanna see the landlord."

"She sees him coming, she'll run a mile."

"And so will Ajay!! Glad she's not in his life anymore."

"Life outside the law!" she says, making eyes. "We're *bad!*"

We catch our breath and my eyes take their always amazed journey across her body. She watches me watching her. She breaths in sharply, runs like a ripple across her broad, young body. Her neck dips a little, until she turns quickly the inch it takes to meet my eye. There's a kiss on her lips, mine to take, a daydream dances on her eyes...

The screen goes pink. I see a beautiful place, instantly. Of her doing, warm radio blooms. And she giggles a little as she watches it traverse my face. I look like a horse that's been given an injection of some choice tranquilliser. He goes weak at the knees and his eyes roll back in his head. I tidy it up, but it's leaked all over the room.

I see us together, like figures on a plain, an horizon wide and white as the Arctic but I don't see how we got there, and I don't see how we go on. No footprints from nor hither. Just figures on the ice plain, standing together but trapped on a disc. No tracks.

I'll never get another offer like this, one so perfectly personal. She wants her varied affections to fit together, be in one piece where she can keep an eye on them.

It's not what she thinks it is, not what she's calling it.

It becomes cold and I realise that I am breathing deeply, breathing in the detergent.

No more than a moment has passed.

It's a matter of imagination.

My phone rings, in Angela's pocket and she responds. We disassemble.

It's the locksmith, Terry, downstairs...

"You missing a TV by any chance, Guv?"

"Nah. Everything's right where I want it."

Angela's eyes flick onto mine.

"Job's on the front door. I'll be down."

"You remember what was said, Yeah?"

"I remember. Yeah."

I peer at the phone shortsightedly, as if it were an alien instrument, like old people do. The line remained open while I took longer than I needed to figure the "No" button.

Angela's thumbs were poked in the pockets of her jeans. She looked down, she was chewing her inner cheek. Her eyes slide up to catch mine, fall...

"Well, that's that," I say, and turn around and walk away.

I turn to see her standing.

"C'mon, sweetheart," I say. "You don't want to be here, do you."

"No," she says, sulkily. "No, I don't."

"Let's go."

"Yeah."

She goes to her flat. I turn down the stair.

"Seeya," she says, looking down her mother's hall.

"Yeah," I say, "Seeya, sweetheart."

Sheep on hill pasture

Robert Davidson

The grass is sweetening and the wind less like a bite.
It's okay to climb. Nothing is stopping her.

It's okay to wander. She can go where the grass takes her.
She has her lambs in pairs, dropping them where she stands.

A sister sheep drags a broken leg.
Another drags a half-birth.

There are corpses on the hill.
There are crows. There are foxes.

Big hands grasp her two right legs and flip her over
to unzip her along the underside and strip her naked.
A foot pushes her off but, back on the hill again,
she forgets all this against the presence of now.

Beyond the passage of days she does not know time.
What she does know is grass, rocks, wind, fear,
soaking, murderous rain, a deep cough, deer passing,

brief maternal love,
brief maternal grief,

the dogs, the men, the van, the humane killer.

Theater

Jennifer K Dick

During exploratory surgery a man finds an ink-black octopus
spread over the heart, a box with an ivy-covered ring. Gilding glints

under fluorescent. A woman is leaning forward in a rocking chair
to untangle a knot from her knitting when her heart skips. A child

gasps and leaps into blue air on a dock, spotting a gold and red fin
in silky murk. Somewhere a line extends, if only to catch.

A silk thread opens at the end of an invisible needle in the body,
cobalt liquid passes into an organ while the victim smiles, leans

close to the woman he is hoping to make love to after dinner. She
smells of petunias, and green seasides. Her gaze is opalescent.

Sky dim as forests shadow a girl's brow. She penetrates
into the underbrush chasing a red fox. A violet just bloomed

in the cool dark. When he takes her hand he is unafraid,
surrounded by the crystalline clink of china, restaurant silver.

Radiant, the surgeon cups his hand round
over the back of the octopus, forming a shell.

Life model

Andrew Dilger

Shelving its silent weight
of bone and blood
a horse sleeps standing up,
with muscles locked.
Too tired to dream
today I do the same.

It takes strength to keep still,
to let the callipers close on
shoulders, thigh, pit of the neck –
the tension, then the touch
as measurements are clutched
like hot coals pincered from the fire.

It takes strength not to stare. Look,
my life is slowly turning into earth:
arms and legs of mud
are moulded over stumps of mild steel
and a face emerges from the fisted clay,
a swimmer surfacing.

Each part has a secret pain
but for a week, then a month I don't speak,
hardly exist except in shape and silhouette.
A chalk outline of feet marks where I've been –
that, and a replica robed like a bride
in polythene.

Black cowboy hat

BR Dionysius

The terrible confession I told my brother
after coffee liqueur rum prised open tongues,
of how I lost our father's black cowboy hat
on a juvenile film set, so civil war, his bull-
riding legacy captured only in a few frames
of grainy betamax. A format outcast too;
our 20th century masculine daguerreotype.
This news tempered on learning that,
nothing in my brother's worldly possessions
belonged to our dad, not beer opener, not
bob watch, bathrobe, tie or boomerang key
ring did he have. So, on him I pinned the
National Service medal & gave our father
some time, newly minted with his son.

Gemini

Isobel Dixon

Below my heart hang two pale women,
ghostly, gelid, sea-horse girls.
Without my telling you would never
see them, tiny tapioca clumps suspended
in the silt between my bones.

So nearly motionless, they are both breathing,
dreaming their amœbic dreams,
and I swear when I wake before dawn, try
vainly to return to mine, I hear them, faintly,
murmuring. But my ribs make a shallow hull

and one of them must go. Duck, bail out,
flushed into the sewage and the wider sea.
I can't endure them both, adrift
among my vital parts, sizing each other up
with tadpole eyes. I must decide

and feed the lucky one. Let the other shrink,
dissolve back to the body's salty soup.
Look closely at them: soulmates, secret
sharers, not-quite-siamese. Who stays,
who goes, which one of them is history?

She kicks up an almighty storm, makes
waves, enormous, tidal; while her sister's
calm, pacific, dull. Our oil-on-troubled-water-
pourer, keeper of the peace. You choose –
mark one who should be squeezed out

of this narrow vessel; voided, spilled,
to lighten, buoy me, make some space.
Plain sailing then, I'll forge ahead, forget
her spectral presence, and a lifetime's
sly, subversive whispering. Learn

single-mindedness at last. But when it's well
and truly done, how will I know? Will I feel
relief, release, how the balance shifts
and settles; then walk straight, unpuzzled,
sure – or limp and stumble, still
obscurely troubled, phantom-limbed?

Flea circus

Antony Dunn

When the time came we packed up the Big Top,
stowed it in the trunk and drove off the map.

Back in the dark the glass tent came alive:
trapeze and cannon, plunge-pool and high-wire,

everything shaken to a frenzied show.
And though we'd later accuse – come to blows –

we'd never be sure which of our number
left the Top unhooked; by trick or blunder

let our stars seize the chance, make a clean jump
out through the countless non-doors of the trunk.

But fled they were, for sure, when we arrived.
And though we made the best of it, and thrived,

found ourselves skilled in micro-mechanics,
some of us resented living off tricks

and felt in the itch of our bad-feeling
the bite of our great hope's flight, the bleeding,

the drop-by-drop drain of a life gone thin.
The fleas, somehow, still, get under our skin.

Blood of a mole

Zdravka Evtimova

Few customers visit my shop, perhaps three or four a day. They look at the animals in the cages but seldom buy them. The room is narrow and there's no room for me behind the counter, so I usually sit on my old moth-eaten chair behind the door. I stare for hours at the frogs, lizards, snakes and insects wriggling under thick, yellowish plates of glass. Teachers come and get frogs for their biology lessons; fishermen drop in to buy bait; that is practically it. Soon, I'll have to close my shop and I'll be sorry; the sleepy, gloomy smell of formalin has always given me peace and an odd feeling of home. I have worked here for five years now.

One day a strange, small woman entered my room. Her face was frightened and grey. She approached me, her arms trembling and as pale as dead white fish in the darkness. The woman did not look at me or say anything. She staggered, reaching for support on the wooden counter. She didn't look like she'd come to buy lizards and snails; perhaps she had simply felt unwell and was looking for help at the first open door she happened to notice. I was afraid she'd fall, and took her by the hand. She remained silent and rubbed her lips with a handkerchief. I was at a loss; it was very quiet and dark in the shop.

"Do you have moles?" she suddenly asked. Then I saw her eyes. They were like old, torn cobwebs, the pupil a little spider in the centre.

"Moles?" I had to tell her I'd never sold moles in the shop and I'd never seen one in my life. The woman wanted to hear something else – an affirmation. I knew it by her eyes, by the timid fingers that reached out to touch me. I felt uneasy staring at her.

"I have no moles," I said. She turned to go, silent and crushed, her head drooping. Her steps were short and uncertain.

"Hey, wait!" I shouted. "Maybe I have some moles." I don't know why I did it. Her body jerked, there was pain in her eyes. I felt bad because I couldn't help her.

"The blood of a mole can cure sick people," she whispered. "You only have to drink three drops."

I was scared. I could feel something evil lurking in the darkness.

"It eases the pain at least," she went on dreamily, her voice thinning into a sob.

"Are you ill?" I asked. The words tore through the thick moist air and made her body shake. "I'm sorry."

"My son is ill."

Her transparent eyelids masked a faint, desperate glitter. Her hands lay numb on the counter, lifeless as firewood. Her narrow shoulders looked narrower in her frayed grey coat.

"A glass of water will make you feel better," I said.

She remained motionless and when her fingers grabbed the glass her eyelids were still closed. She turned to go, small and frail, her back hunched, her steps noiseless and impotent in the dark. I ran after her. I had made up my mind.

"I'll give you blood of a mole!" I shouted.

The woman stopped in her tracks and covered her face with her hands. It was unbearable looking at her. I felt empty. I didn't have any mole's blood. I didn't have any moles. I imagined the woman in the room, sobbing. Perhaps she was still holding her face in her hands. Well, I closed the door so that she could not see me, then I cut my left wrist with a knife. The wound bled and slowly oozed into a little glass bottle. After ten drops had covered the bottom, I ran back to the room where the woman was waiting.

"Here it is," I said. "Here's the blood of a mole."

She said nothing, just stared at my left wrist. The wound was still bleeding slightly, so I shoved my arm under my apron. The woman glanced at me and kept silent. She didn't reach for the glass bottle; instead, she turned and hurried to the door. I overtook her and forced the bottle into her hands.

"It's blood of a mole!"

She fingered the transparent bottle. The blood inside sparkled like dying fire. Then she took some money out of her pocket.

"No. No," I said.

Her head hung low. She threw the money on the counter without a word. I wanted to accompany her to the corner. I even poured another glasss of water, but she wouldn't wait. The shop was empty again and the lizards' eyes glittered like wet pieces of broken glass.

Cold, uneventful days slipped by. The autumn leaves whirled hopelessly in the wind; the air was brown. The early winter blizzards hurled snowflakes against the windows and sang in my veins. I couldn't forget the woman. I'd lied to her. No one entered my shop, and in the quiet dusk I tried to imagine what her son looked like. The ground was frozen, the streets deserted and the winter had tied its icy knot around houses, souls and rocks.

One morning, the door of my shop opened abruptly. The same small grey woman entered, and before I had time to greet her, she rushed and embraced me. Her shoulders were weightless and frail, and tears streaked her delicately wrinkled cheeks. Her body was shaking. I thought she'd collapse, so I caught her trembling arms. Then the woman grabbed my left hand and lifted it up to her eyes. The scar had vanished, but she found the place. Her lips kissed my wrist, and her tears warmed my skin.

"He can walk!" The woman sobbed, hiding a tearful smile behind her palms. "He can walk!"

She wanted to give me money; her big black bag was full of things she had brought for me. I accompanied her to the corner, but she only stayed there beside the streetlamp, looking at me, small and smiling in the cold.

It was so cosy in my dark shop and the old, faint smell of formalin made me dizzy with happiness. My lizards were so beautiful – I loved them like they were my own children.

In the afternoon of that same day, a strange man entered my room. He was tall, scraggly and frightened.

"Have you... the blood of a mole?" he asked, his eyes piercing. I was scared.

"No, I haven't. I've never sold moles here."

"Oh, you have! You have! Three drops... three drops, no more... My wife will die. You have! Please!"

He squeezed my arm.

"Please... three drops! Or she'll die..."

My blood trickled slowly from the wound. The man held a little bottle and the red drops gleamed in it like embers. Then the man left and a little bundle of bank-notes rolled on the counter.

The following morning a great, whispering mob of strangers waited in front of my door. Their hands clutched little glass bottles.

"Blood of a mole! Blood of a mole!"

They shouted, shrieked, and pushed each other. Each had a sick person at home and a knife in his hand.

Italian masturbazione

Peter Finch

The orgasm is one of the more intense pleasures that can be tried
even if of short duration. He seems natural to try to have of the greater
possible number through the sexual relationships or with
the masturbazione. I even try to procurarsi the pleasure with
the masturbazione without to be involved with other persons.

I do not understand why one must limit when this is easy to obtain
and innocuous for the health. I do not eat manicaretti and leccornie
all days which in the long run can nuocere my health,
but I do try to have the greater number of orgasms
(also resorting to the masturbazione)
the pleasure that it gives to me is intense.

I am astonished that all are not behaved like me.
When then I feel the women that they consider the degrading
masturbazione and therefore to avoid, the arms fall off me.
Is there is something that does not go in this my way to think?

Memorial

David Finkle

I.

Not to put too maudlin a point on it, but there is a stretch of Back Street inhabited by gay men. I know about the well-shaded part of town because on a couple of occasions in the past I've held short-term leases on apartments there.

I hadn't thought about this for a long time but was reminded a month or so ago when I reached the *Times* obituary page – I haven't yet gotten to that point in life when the obits are what I open to first, but soon, soon – and saw a notice for Noah Goodman's memorial service. Noah Goodman used to visit me on Back Street, and I used to visit him on Easy Street. Not that any of his neighbors – figurative or otherwise – knew anything about it.

Anyway I'll drop the metaphor and stick to the facts and feelings as they returned to me, overcame me, during the course of that memorial service, which I did attend. An affair at which upwards of one hundred others also appeared – none of whom I knew but some of whom I knew about. A woman called Rosalind Paynter (I actually had encountered her in quite another context long after Noah and I had all but lost touch) presided at the event and, in the course of her opening remarks, said something like "I expect each of you will remember exactly where you met Noah, because he always made such an impact."

Like so many who spoke about him in the dimmed auditorium that noontime, she was absolutely right. I certainly remembered exactly where I met Noah: at the Turtle Bay Baths. The summer of 1974. A muggy July night, to be even more specific. (None of the speakers commemorating him recalled a similar meeting.) Did he wander into my cubicle and grab my dick? Did I amble into his roomette and trail the fingers of one hand along his hairy calf? Did we catch each other's eye in the showers? Or pass one another in a busy corridor amid all the libidinous coming-and-goings? That I don't remember. I assume we joined up, possibly without speaking at all, in some time-honored way (ironically, rituals at the baths were rigid, considering the supposed liberated setting). Either before, during and/or after engaging in illicit activity, we must have fallen into a conversation during which we became intrigued enough to go home together.

To Noah's home – the snug apartment described accurately by one of Noah's other eulogists as "so full of books you couldn't get from the front door to the nearest chair or from one room to the next without running the risk of upsetting four-foot high stacks of book." Books, I'll add, of every shape and category. Books with fresh, slick jackets and books bound in crumbling, tooled leather. Books spiked with bookmarks or bits of paper. Books lying open and upside down one on another. Books never likely to come under the tyranny of anyone's decimal system.

On my entering that unusual library, it wasn't the stacks that fell, however; I was what fell. A sucker for books, for reading, for volumes and tomes as insignias of erudition, I took one sweeping glance around the small living-room (I guessed that's what it must be because I thought I caught a glimpse of a leather divan under one especially large-ish and wide-ish pile of books) and told myself I'd hit pay dirt. I'd met the kind of man I'd always wanted to meet, a man who loves books as much as I do. More. Enough to give them the run of the place, which I, in my fastidiousness, could never quite allow myself to do.

The movie in my head cuts to us in Noah's single bed (single brass bed) an hour or so later and Noah saying, "I love you." This with a clarion ring that matched the brightness of the brass posts. This after our having been together so briefly it's possible we were still unsure of each other's first name. Of course, I knew he didn't love me – much the opposite, was exposing suspicious impetuosity by saying that he did love me on such short acquaintance. (If you could even stretch our brief meeting far enough to call it an acquaintance.) Yet I thought, while he had his arms around me, while he was looking at me with that gaze only the newly- or recently-infatuated can conjure, that maybe he could come to love me, that his saying he already did – intelligent man that he clearly was – was his way of declaring not that he truly loved me but that he expected he could, that he was announcing his intention to give it the old college try.

So there I was – with the four a.m. moonlight falling through the narrow window of his narrow bedroom onto the narrow bed we were so eager to be uncomfortable in – deciding I was happy because I'd found a man who was going to love me and whom I expected I could love back. And so we fell into the fitful sleep of the carelessly charmed.

Morning came. Noah got up, said little, went to the kitchen, came back with two glasses of orange juice and a book of Wallace Stevens's collected poems. Don't you know he read me the very poem someone read during the memorial service? Someone who knew, as I had learned, that this was Noah's favorite poem. Well, one of his favorites (he'd waffle when asked to commit): 'The anecdote of the jar'. Noah looked around for his rimless glasses, located them somewhere near the bed, put them on without entirely hooking them behind his ears. "I placed a jar upon a hill/And round it was..." His tones as he read were deep and sonorous yet marked by, had at their center, a humor, a lightness, a – what? – a young man's buoyancy. (When we met, Noah was 48, and I was 34.) He finished reading, shut the book, put it on the window sill, took his glasses off, folded the earpieces, placed them on top of the book. "Wonderful, isn't it?" I agreed it was, though I wasn't certain I entirely understood it; am still not sure. I said, "Read another one." "Oh, no, beamish boy," Noah replied, getting up, "With poems of that caliber you only read one, and then you think about it for a long time." He took a couple of steps towards the bathroom. "I'm going in here to think. I'll leave you to do your thinking exactly where you are." He took another step, turned around just before closing the door, "Are you thinking?" He was grinning widely; Noah had a great grin, a grin that could light the world. "I'm thinking, I'm thinking," I said, recalling Jack Benny's joke response to the robber's threat, "Your money or your life." "Good Benny," Noah said and shut the bathroom door behind him. When he came out, he barely looked at me, just picked up his glasses and the Wallace Stevens poems and passed through to the living-room. I could hear him moving around. I thought maybe I was still supposed to be thinking about 'The anecdote of the jar'. Instead, I wondered whether I was at the beginning or the end of something. My romantic history would indicate the latter.

A few minutes went by, and Noah appeared in the bedroom door. Dressed. Not well-dressed – he was never what you'd call well-dressed. But dressed. A tweed jacket (keep in mind it was July); an Oxford shirt with a very thin regimental tie (keep in mind wide ties with all sorts of tie-dye prints were the fashion in 1974). "Do you want any breakfast?" he asked. I couldn't tell whether yes or no was required. "Well, I – uh..." "If you do, there's cereal in a cabinet over the sink in the kitchen. Anything else you need is approximately where you'd expect it to be. When you're ready to go, just let yourself out." I was startled. "Are you leaving?" He looked at me as if I'd asked an extremely stupid question. "I'm due at my office. I make a habit of getting there on time. Punctuality is the politeness of bosses."

I roused myself from the bed, confused and a little angry. "Wait a minute," I said, reaching around for the clothes I'd dropped (as instructed the previous night) on a pile of books. "I'll leave with you." "No hurry." I was not at all pleased at the idea of being left alone in what was still a stranger's apartment. I felt what I was getting was a rather creative heave-ho. "Stay as long as you like," Noah said and took a little pause. "I want to see you again, of course, but I'm just not sure when I'll be able to. I'm very busy. I've got your phone number." He went to the front door, opened it, turned and smiled in a way that said he was only doing what he felt he probably should. "The front door will lock behind you automatically." He left. I'd been co-opted. I had given him my number the night before when we were discussing leaving the baths together but hadn't yet concluded we would. Now he'd said he'd call when he was free; what I heard implicitly – but clearly – was, don't call me first. Exasperated, one-upped, I looked around at the books, thought about the day in front of me, wondered whether I might as well just fix myself something to eat.

At the time I'm writing about I had only recently left a full-time job. A small inheritance had come to me unexpectedly when a favorite aunt died. Who would ever have guessed she'd saved so much money? My father would have been the one to know, and even he was surprised. As a matter of fact, how she amassed her impressive nest-egg had become a matter of much speculation in the family. Had there been a rich lover? A winning lottery ticket? Would an embezzlement charge be slapped on her posthumously? Dinner conversation with my parents and brothers when we got together once, twice a month had become each of us breaking the others up as we took turns spinning wilder and wilder tales of how Aunt Esther made her millions. (It wasn't millions; it was considerably less, but still enough to delight the nieces and nephews she'd smiled on from beyond the grave.)

So having given myself a year to write the novel I'd always said I'd write if only I had a year to write a novel, I was edging into a routine in fits and starts. Time on my hands: I'd never been good with it. With no reason, then, to race home that July morning I took Noah up on his offer, poured myself out a bowl of bran flakes (bowl and flakes found where Noah said they would be) and another glass of orange juice, went onto his terrace (Noah lived 16 floors above lower Manhattan with, I'd estimate, a 240-degree view) and sat down to think. I don't remember what I thought.

Truth to tell, up to that point in my life I'd never been much of a thinker. More precisely, I knew my mother was right when she said, as she often did, "You've got a good head on your shoulders." It's just that I wasn't inclined to use it more than I absolutely had to. In situations where thinking might have served me well, I frequently did anything but. The notion, for instance, of taking mental inventory or putting options in perspective when an unread issue of *People* magazine was at hand carried no weight with me. I avoided thinking, brushed off anything that went beyond superficial considerations of who and where I was. So the chances are I avoided any kind of meaningful thought that morning on Noah's terrace. I paged through a handful of books I'd brought out to skim over breakfast, looked cursorily around at the sunlit panorama, maybe even counted water towers since I happen to love water towers and judge the quality of high-rise apartments by the number of water towers that can be seen from them.

I wouldn't want to be held to it, but my guess is that during this perfectly nice interval I decided I shouldn't expect much more from Noah, that the impassioned proclamations of the previous night were no more than standard heat-of-the-moment lies just more cleverly phrased than most. I probably concluded that what was left me at that point were whatever luxurious minutes I could wring out of my sit on that metropolitan version of a front porch. I leafed through some books, read parts of them, perused the notes Noah had made in the margins. (He'd made many, in an angular, back-slanted hand. On one page of a dog-eared copy of Kant's *Prolegomena* he'd inscribed "Poppycock, Immie!") When an hour or so got idled away, I finished dressing, washed out the glass and bowl I'd used, thought about but didn't write a thank-you-for-the-use-of-the-hall note and left. The door did indeed lock behind me automatically.

II.

Noah called me that afternoon somewhere between three or four. I was surprised but something told me – rightly? – not to let on. "What are you doing tonight?" he asked in an enthusiastic voice I not only recognized but to which I could already affix a facial expression. "I don't know. Tonight? Nothing." "We're going to Gage & Tollner. I'll come by at 6:15." "Sure. Okay. Sure. Fine." A silence: Gage & Tollner meant nothing to me. "Do you have my address?" "Yes." I didn't remember telling him. "Did I give it to you?" "No." "How'd you get it?" (These were the days when my defenses shot up if I thought someone homosexual knew where I lived and might drop in on me without my wanting him to. Still somewhat homophobic myself, I had paranoid fears that I might put myself in a situation where the vice squad or, worse, gay-bashers wielding baseball bats would show up at my door in the middle of the night and drag me into the street while neighbors in bathrobes stood around astonished to learn that the nice-enough fellow downstairs was, would you believe it, nothing but a garden variety cocksucker.) "Calme-toi, amigo," he said. "You're in the phone book." Imagine my embarrassment. "I'll see you at 6:15." "Okay." "Aren't you going to ask me why 6:15, not 6 or 6:30?" "I will if you like." "In *The prime of Jean Brodie* – the movie; I don't know about the book – the headmistress asks Jean Brodie to come to her office at 2:45, and Jean Brodie says to somebody or another, 'She thinks to intimidate me by the use of quarter hours.' Ever since I heard it, I think to intimidate people by the use of quarter hours." "I'm not intimidated." "I know. That's why I love you." There. He'd said it again. I realized I didn't mind hearing it.

Gage & Tollner is a well-known – though it wasn't to me – restaurant on Fulton Street in downtown Brooklyn. We went by subway. As we rode out, Noah told me how much he liked the place and that, though it was not exactly one of those off-the-beaten-track beaneries whose secret regulars guard tenaciously, he didn't go out of his way to introduce just anyone to it. How did he know it was the sort of venue where I'd feel completely comfortable, that the dark, carved wood was right up my æsthetic alley, that the chandeliers with candles flickering in them and the four-square food made me want to jump up and click my heels in the air? The answer is: he didn't know. He suspected; he hoped; he put me to the test. He was saying without saying: this is the kind of thing I like; if you don't, so much for you. He was saying: I think we like the same things; I want to find out immediately, because if we're not on the same wavelength, there's no use wasting my time or yours.

I passed the test. I let Noah order – nothing fancy, sole *meunière*, potatoes, corn-on-the-cob, ginger ale. The food was fine, the dinner conversation had to do with his day and mine. Well, less with mine, since, as I say, I was trying to establish a routine and – I still used a typewriter then – was full of going through the time-honored motions of being a writer (gazing at half-typed pages, pulling them from the roller in big gestures, crumpling them, tossing them at the wastebasket). I'd finished the first drafts of several chapters of something I wasn't ready to call a novel. For reasons I'm about to explain, as dinner went on, I was even less inclined to say much about what I was doing. Noah, you see, was a publisher – no surprise, of course, what with all the books. But he hadn't said a great deal about his work the night before, and what he had said – during an obligatory and cursory exchange of autobiographical information as we reclined on his slightly damp bathhouse mattress – could have meant anything, could have meant he was an editor, a book designer, in sales, in marketing.

Over the perfectly-done sole he was explicit. He headed his own division at an established publishing house. It was a recent development in his life. For years he had been independent. He and his senior year roommate had come out of Harvard with a conviction that what Bennett Cerf and Donald Klopfer had done before them with the Modern Library, they could do with something similar. The war was over; they'd saved a little money; they went to Europe to track down authors in France, Italy, the Netherlands, Austria, even some of the Balkan countries (the politics were sticky) who weren't yet being published in English because of "esoteric subject matter," "limited appeal." The two Charles River boys showed up on foreign stoops flashing high-wattage grins and working the naivete Europeans so often expect from and patronize in Americans. They offered their prey small advances for exclusive publishing rights in the United States; they promised solid translations and stylish production; they hedged on their plans for distribution – here language barriers were on their side.

You, of course, have realized now why the name Noah Goodman sounds so familiar – if it does. He's one-half of Youngerman & Goodman. That's right, he is the Noah Goodman. He is the Noah Goodman who was the first to publish in this country so many household names and, in a couple of instances, Nobel prize winners. His house and his reputation grew, and, as he reported it while slathering butter on corn, so did the headaches. Things between him and Stanton Youngerman – never all that copacetic – worsened over time until they both agreed it would be a relief to sell to a larger house and be subsumed into operations there; Goodman got his house, Youngerman his. So far, so mezz-a-mezz was his estimation: he'd been his own boss for so long, it was not comfortable for him to be told by others what he could be doing to improve grosses.

Skipping names of the famous into our conversation like stones across water, Noah acted as if dealing with men and women whom I knew as syllabus requirements was, for him, all in a day's work. Needless to say, that's precisely what it was, but it sure took the wind out of my piddling sails. Before Noah had begun to fill in the outlines of his prominence and power in the publishing world, I had made a few tentative remarks about writing a novel. But the more he said about himself, the less inclined I was to offer more about myself." Why? Let's see: one, I suddenly felt that talking about my whatever-it-was-I-was-writing was somehow placing myself in competition with the major and minor classics he'd championed, a competition I wasn't ever likely to win. And two, I suspected there would be trouble if a potential second agenda become entangled in our whatever-it-was-we-were-doing. So by the time we got around to dessert I had backed away so gingerly from defining my project I had all but reduced it to a short comedy skit I was doodling with for my own amusement. I parried his tell-me-about-its with so many there's-nothing-to-tells that he finally stopped asking and said, "Whatever you do, you're going to be successful at it." I was so pleased at that – I hadn't fished for it – I felt as if a light had been turned on inside me, but, as was often my inclination, I was immediately sceptical. Noah, of course, had just presented impressive credentials for predicting achievement, but then again he had read nothing of mine, nor, I took note, did he go so far as to ask whether he could. "How do you know I'll succeed?" I begged gracelessly. "It's what I'm paid to know. It's the only talent I have. So shut up and let me exercise it."

Thus ended a subject I saw to it never came up again.

When dinner was over, Noah remarked that, though he'd admired my apartment when he'd come by to collect me and quite liked the way I'd decorated and lived in it, he'd prefer to go back to his. Said with the silky politeness of a man used to doing things his way: "If you're absolutely sure you don't mind..." I didn't: those books. Back we went, where, on entering, Noah went to the stereo set and put a record on. "Do you know this?" he asked when the first strains of a piano piece I didn't know batted the air around. It was a piece which – no coincidence, of course – was cited by one of the grieving speakers at the memorial service. Noah must have played it for, or at least discussed it with, many of his friends: Beethoven's 'Hammerklavier' Sonata. I'd never heard it before, or didn't remember having ever heard it. We settled – as near as anyone could settle – into two of Noah's reading chairs and listened in silence. Noah with his elbows on the uncomfortable wooden arms of the chair in which he was sitting. He rested his head against the fingers of his hands and rose only to turn the record over. Otherwise he remained immobile.

The sonata ended and, without bothering to speak or turn off the amplifier, he took my hand and led me to the bedroom. Again we had sex. "I love you," Noah said among many unintelligible guttural sounds. "I love you." I wondered whether I was expected to reciprocate; decided I wasn't. So I lay back and enjoyed myself as much as I could, which was a great deal. But not absolutely. The problem was mine (low-level but undeniable embarrassment over homosexual nookie) and his. I felt he still had no right to say what he insisted on saying: "I love you." We slept again, and again we woke. Again Noah dressed hurriedly – was he wearing the same clothes he'd worn the day before or were they merely identical? – and left me to use the apartment as I wanted. Again he rushed out saying he couldn't be sure when he would be able to see me again. The door locked automatically behind him.

I was less surprised when he called later that day and said he wanted to see the David Rabe play at Lincoln Center people were talking about, that he'd taken the liberty of reserving two tickets for that night. Could I meet him there at 7:45? "I'm still not intimidated by the use of quarter hours," I said. When Noah laughed, it was with all the joy of an audience watching the Marx Brothers in *A Night at the Opera*.

III.

That's how it began, and that's the way it continued for the rest of the summer. Mornings, on leaving his apartment – rarely, indeed I think never, mine – Noah would peal off some version of his expecting to see me again but uncertain when. The inevitable follow-up phone call laying out the evening's plans came between three and four, and I was home or I wasn't. Usually I was, plugging away at the typewriter or staring vacantly over it. (I'd settled on a novel about a man who decides to die for love, literally.) On weekends we toured the city. Let's see, what would have been a typical event? Well, there was the Saturday morning Noah called and said, "Drop everything – not your drawers, dummy! – we're going to the Met." He came by in a cab, ferried me uptown where we took the outside stairs of the Metropolitan Museum of Art two at a time, paid our suggested donations and made a beeline to the mediæval hall. There he went up to the carving of a lady saint and said, "There she is!" "She," according to the card on the plinth, was a Lindenwood reliquary bust of Saint Barbara, the patroness of firemen and architects. (She'd been incarcerated in a tower by her jealous father and then beheaded when, to the two windows already in place in her tower, she added a third in honor of the Holy Trinity.) The unnamed sculptor – "School of Nicoleus Gerhært von Leyden" – had given her a narrow, high-browed face framed by long, thick, fluid strawberry-blonde tresses. She wore a modest crown and a prim, purse-lipped expression. With her right hand she had her thumb and forefinger poised as if indicating a fraction-of-an-inch measure, and with her left hand she cradled a burnt-sienna model of the tower in which she'd been jailed by her vengeful father. "What do you think?" Noah asked. I thought. "She's beautiful," I said, "But sour." "Ah-hah," Noah snapped, "That's what I thought you'd say." He dropped to his haunches. "Now look." I dropped to my haunches and gazed up at the saint, who suddenly appeared not pinched but reassuringly serene, the kind of heavenly figure you might imagine would instill belief in frightened 15th century souls. "You see," Noah said, "she was meant to be seen from below. Whoever the genius was who carved her knew what he was doing." We admired her some more on our haunches. "Remarkable, isn't it?" Noah asked.

Other times, not on our haunches, we attended plays, movies, concerts. We aired opinions about them from the minute the curtain descended (the last credit faded, the conductor lay down his baton) until long after we'd returned to

Noah's apartment. Often when we got back, we'd be in the midst of some disagreement that needed settling. Before anything got done, a kettle put on the burner, a brandy poured, a mound of ice cream dished out, Noah would quick-step to a bookshelf to find corroborating proof of whatever argument he'd been making. Sometimes the substantiating book was where he expected it to be; sometimes it wasn't and he'd have to search through pile after pile, knocking them over, leaving the books exactly as they fell. Whether he found what he was looking for immediately or whether it took a half hour, his action when he finally put his hand on the sought book was the same. He'd smile – have I mentioned he had dimples in both cheeks? – with the vindictive triumph of someone who's just won a rancorous debate (the arrogance, I'd think lovingly) and say, as he'd said at Saint Barbara's side, "Ah hah!" Was he always right? Was I always wrong? I don't remember. My best recollection is that he was right more often than I. Even though what we'd been contending then is lost to me now, I can still feel the ignominy of having been trumped.

Wait: I remember one battle. It had to do with a Shakespeare sonnet. Oh, which is it? 'Sonnet 73', the one beginning, "That time of year thou mayst in me behold…" For some reason it had come up in response to something we'd seen or heard earlier that night. We were quarreling over the second line. I insisted it went, "When yellow leaves, or few, or none, do hang…"; Noah said it went, "When yellow leaves, or none, or few, do hang…" (I didn't say these arguments weren't free of pedantry.) I maintained one of the reasons I remembered the line so precisely was that the progression of the number of yellow leaves from few to none lent an exquisite dying rhythm. Had Shakespeare put "none" before "few," the line would be choppy, unsatisfying, would lack its amazing grace. "Beamish boy," Noah said, "but that's Shakespeare. He's conversational when you expect him to be poetic. I'll rephrase that. Shakespeare finds the poetry in conversation. In discourse. He confounds expectation. Come to mention it, I can't think of a better definition of genius: the gift of confounding expectation." You're wrong about this, I insisted. You'll see I'm not, he countered. "Okay, wise guy," I said when we'd gotten to the apartment. "Let me show you where you're wrong – I'm going to love this." I snatched The Complete Works of Shakespeare, which he had just ah-hahed over locating, and opened as quickly as I could to 'Sonnet 73': "That time of year thou mayst in me behold/When yellow leaves, or none, or few, do hang…" Foiled again.

Perhaps I remember this incident because there was a second lesson for me beneath the lesson in Shakespearean technique. The lesson was about me. I was the sort of person who too often expected the expected, was so used to adhering to what was expected that even when it wasn't there, I still saw or heard or smelled or tasted it. Whereas Noah, always on the lookout for genius, found it in the unexpected. He never pointed out this disparity between us to me, may never have even been inclined to. But the way I see things it accounts in some measure for what was to come.

Not that Noah's life was a string of uninterrupted small triumphs overshadowing my uninterrupted series of minor mis-steps. He had his downs. One bright morning when I was sitting outside drinking in the new day – and orange juice – I became aware that he was standing at the terrace door. I had the impression he'd been there for some time. Maybe not. I'd thought he was still in the bathroom shaving. He continued standing there, not focusing on me – not looking directly at anything as near as I could tell. "I don't recognize my face," he said. I was puzzled and probably would have appeared so had he focused on me. "I look in the mirror. I don't know myself anymore. I look at my face, and it's not the face I remember."

I realize I haven't given much, or any, physical description of Noah. Now, I think, is as good a time as any. That morning, in the door, wearing unpressed brown trousers, unshined cordovan shoes, a white t-shirt puckered with age, Noah stood five feet ten, had thick, hairy, inordinately long arms that hung from his shoulders like parentheses, a thick chest, a medicine ball belly. His lined face was basically an inverted triangle. He had straight gray hair he parted on the left and kept long in the front so that it fell over his eyes. Sometimes, not often, he combed it back with his meaty fingers. His eyes were deep-set and dark under bushy salt-and-pepper eyebrows. They gave him a look that would have been grave had he not leavened it with those raucous laughs. I've said that his smile was radiant. His teeth weren't, the bottom ones discolored by coffee and tobacco.

I wasn't falling in love – hadn't fallen in love – with Noah for his looks, however. When I told friends about him, which I must have done, I'm sure I never described him as handsome. In truth, I thought he was plain, homely even. What I liked in him was something else entirely. And yet when said he didn't recognize himself, something in me shifted; I – who, of course, did recognize Noah's face as the face he'd had since I'd known him – instantly understood that he was handsome. No, that's not quite it. I understood he had been quite handsome, and if I looked closely, as he was trying to do with evident difficulty, I would be able to see through to the young man he'd been. I'd be able to see the 15-year-old Noah who – during the war – attracted, as he'd told me a number of times, soldiers to his side in Greenwich Village homosexual bars. Suddenly I could do what Noah couldn't; in the harsh morning light I could see him with the years stripped away. I thought, how awful to lose yourself, the self you knew; I thought, how far off is the morning when I will look in the mirror and see a stranger there? I said nothing to Noah. I didn't know what to say. He remained where he was for a few more seconds, then shrugged his simian-like shoulders and arms, turned and went back inside.

Another evening much later in the summer Noah, seated in the carved straight back chair he used for reading – well, he used anything for reading – got to talking about what he was looking for in a man with whom he could truly, deeply fall in love and with whom he could stay that way. Without saying so in that many words, he made it clear I wasn't the man. True, he had told me he loved me numerous times, but the frequency of his saying so was in indirect proportion to the length of time we spent together. On the surface little had changed. If anything, our romance was maturing into something approximating the comfort of devoted marrieds. The plays, movies, concerts we'd gone to nightly at the beginning of the affair now alternated with entire nights passed at home – his place or mine. We made love, experimented. I'd never liked being fucked but went along with it a few times. (Once after Noah'd fucked me, I went to take a piss and noticed blood in my urine. My stray thought was, I'd been deflowered; today, in the age of AIDS, it would be a scarier reaction.)

Noah rediscovered that he loved to cook. He hadn't cooked regularly for some time. He had no reason to. He disliked cooking for himself. But now he found he enjoyed paging through his mother's cookbooks for favorite recipes, got immense pleasure from rattling pots and pans, liked making roasts, loved fooling around with seasonings, was all but addicted to corn-on-the-cob. (In for the evening or out, we had corn every night; if out, we called ahead to make sure the restaurant we would be patronizing served fresh corn.) The nights we were at his house, was I allowed to pitch in? "No." "Go sit in the living-room out of harm's way." "Be surprised." "Your job is to gasp with delight when I remove the metal lid." He took great satisfaction in an appreciated meal, liked lolling around afterwards looking pleased with himself, ready on his full stomach to become expansive about anything that came to him or me.

What came up the evening I'm talking about was my trying yet again to pin him down on his attitude towards me. He gave me his answer by defining what he wanted in a dream man. "The man I'll fall in love with for all time," he said, cupping his hands to his left breast, "will fill me with such joy my heart will tip over." He leaned sideways in his chair to illustrate how this overflowing heart would cause him to list. I wanted to say, "And I don't fill your heart to overflowing?" But it was obvious; I didn't.

"I was on a beach once in Biarritz," Noah said, "when I saw a boy who gave me that feeling. He must have been 18 or 19. He had a lean, smooth body. He looked as if he had never been touched. As if he had been delivered from the sea on a shell like Botticelli's Venus. His hair was black. His eyes were a very light blue. Or I imagined they were. He stood for the longest time looking at the horizon. He wasn't more than 15 feet away from me, but I couldn't bring myself to speak to him."

I felt myself getting angry at being told about this unknown boy and also being told by implication that I didn't fit the bill. I thought Noah was being foolishly romantic, ludicrously unrealistic. I stewed, said nothing, smiled as if I were on his side, as if I could see that boy standing at the edge of the ocean, as if I shared in the appreciation of his beauty. But I knew something inside me had been chipped away, something irreparable had happened.

I'd even foreseen it somewhat – my undoing at Noah's hands – in a poem I'd written. And, like a dunce, had read to him. Like a bigger dunce, I'm going to quote it in full here. Not because I think it's very good (it's not, but it also isn't the worst thing I've ever read), but because I recently found it in an old notebook and have decided it gives a fair idea of my frame of mind during that singular summer:

"You see these two fingers," you said and held up the index and middle finger of your left hand.
"If I press down on a certain spot, I can make your toes fall off."
I laughed as if I had never heard anything so silly – or witty.
(Oh, I was so cocky and prone and pleased with you!)
"You don't believe me," you said and applied the finger to points on my back.
Damned if my toes didn't fall off!
"See," you said.
I looked at those pathetic toes, already hard as pebbles, at the foot of the bed.
"And if I press down here," you said and did before I even thought to stop you, "your feet will fall off."
Presto! They swung loose and dropped free, exposing, on my ankles, hinges I'd never noticed before.
"And here and here," you said, your fingers moving rapidly, "your hands and arms."
And now you turned cavalier.
"And if I press my mouth here" – I was powerless to stop you – "your legs and here your ears and nose and chin and here your head."
I was scattered about the room like birdseed.
"Next time – " you said, sweeping up the many pieces of me and sorting them into boxes containing the shriveled parts of anonymous others,
"Next time you'll believe me when I tell you something."
"How can there be a next time," I wanted to ask, but couldn't,
of course, because my lips were where they had rolled,
under the bed, cracked and drying out – Orange rinds in the moonlight.

IV.

Noah began his open-ended trip around the world that December – after we'd been together, if that's what you want to call it, five months. Give or take a week. The official story on his extravagant departure was that he had finally gotten up the gumption to do something he'd talked about doing his entire adult life but kept putting off. The head of a prestigious publishing house, he explained, doesn't have time to troop the planet other than piecemeal, on weekend drop-ins to writers in need of wooing – "three days in Paris for talks over amiable meals and jocular wines, lucky if you get a free hour to breeze through the Louvre," that sort of thing.

But Noah no longer owned a publishing house. He'd sold. Nevertheless, a house, like Noah Goodman Books, within a larger house – where intramural competitions can stir ferocious acquiring tempests – provided even fewer opportunities for setting one's own pace. Dissatisfied with his new set-up practically from the first day that Youngerman & Goodman had been folded into Century and the Goodman imprimatur launched, Noah grew only progressively more hostile to what he'd gotten himself into and progressively more interested in finding a way out. He took a look at his bank account, huddled with his accountant, saw that his salary wasn't a necessity, that the income from his portfolio was enough to cradle him for the rest of his life. So – with a promise to be on call when absolutely needed no matter where he was – he wiped his hands of the mistaken enterprise and handed his authors to Youngerman, whose office at the other end of the floor was actually not much farther away than it'd ever been.

While the sale was in progress, by the way, it wasn't confided to me. I was told when it was a *fait accompli* and in a manner not too far removed from, "By the way, did I happen to mention to you that..?" Actually worse. It came up during a cab ride home (Noah's home in that building hoity-toitily namely after a master painter) from some flashy European director's dismantling of *The cherry orchard*. Noah, whose genius extended to mimicry, segued directly from his send-up of the actress who'd just turned Madame Ranevsky into a Minsk fishwife to informing me that he'd put finishing touches on the itinerary for his upcoming trip – er... um, for the first leg of the trip. "What do you mean I didn't tell you I was going away?" "You never mentioned it." "Of course, I did. I must have. I've been telling everybody." "Not me." "The only thing I can think is that I've told so many people I assumed I must have told you." "You didn't." "I am. Going away. But not immediately, not for ten days."

It was all disingenuous and unworthy of him. Not to say transparent. And once he'd filled me in on the official story, I was able to piece together the unofficial story, which, I didn't bring up then because I couldn't prove my theory and didn't want the humiliation of his scoffing at it. But which I bring up now. Though, with Noah dead, I have even less chance of proving it: Noah had chosen this particular moment in his life to circle the globe on a slow boat because it was the most graceful way he could think of to get away from me. He was framing something negative (throwing me over) as something positive (realizing a deferred dream).

An egocentric interpretation? Okay. I'll rephrase it. Our affair had reached the critical point at which you either go forwards by acknowledging there is a couple here and it's time to start a life together with everything that implies – foremost: introductions all around to friends and possibly even family. Or you go backwards. Remaining in place is spinning wheels. It must have been as clear to him as it was to me. And Noah – used to life in a book-lined closet – was unprepared at his age and given his generation and everything to which he had accustomed himself to go forward. Except perhaps with the elusive fellow of heart-tipping capabilities – wherever that impossible dream was hiding out. Therefore it was obvious he had only one recourse: backing off. But colorfully. To Paris, Cairo, Bangkok, Johannesburg, Hong Kong. I, of course, wasn't the one making him pack his bags. I'm not that sold on myself. I'm convinced anyone who had gotten as close as I had would have forced the same action. I just happened to be the one standing in the wrong place.

Of Noah's departure here's what comes back to me. His extrication from Noah Goodman Books (a series of farewell lunches and parties to which I, of course, wasn't invited) and his preparations to leave (not knowing where he was going, he took shots for everything but bought no new clothes) left us little time to see each other. Or, more exactly, left us with a handy excuse to see little of each other. Meaningfully, we had no declared last dinner. He merely left town after a short phone call during which he promised to be in contact through the mail "or whatever."

And he was. Letters I threw into the drawer of my Mission desk after reading them arrived at sporadic intervals – the longer he was away, the more sporadic. The first was from London sometime in March, 1975. The three, four months that had gone by with no word didn't seem too neglectful to me, considering. He did have to get his traveler's legs. The letter – typed on yellow foolscap – was what I was hoping for, funny and flattering; *Beamish Boy:- Going to theater every night. Getting into trouble because I keep nudging the person next to me at crucial moments. Forget it's not you. Have been slapped by a Mayfair dowager and had my knee squeezed by an Earl's Court homosexual. That's pronounced ha-mah-sex-you-ehl, with an emphasis on the sex. As it should be. Pulled strings, and am now able to use the reading-room at the British Museum. When the tourists come in every hour on the hour to look at the scholars, I'm one of the scholars they look at. I try to oblige by appearing important. But feel a sham. I'm not studying anything. Just testing the stacks. I keep dreaming up books I've always heard about and never seen. So I request them. They show up. I write racy Olde English epithets in the margins and send them back. But the staff is on to me. Tried to sneak the Magna Carta out the other day in a rolled umbrella but was stopped and told in a stern whisper and no uncertain terms by a female book warden, "It simply isn't done." The hotel has central heating but, like all things English, they're too polite to try to impress you with it. Are you writing? I hope so. No one else is. I've been reading some of the young novelists here, and am in a position to know. Love, Noah*

Six months later from Paris: *Garçon Rayonnant:- I have discovered the best food in Paris. The Jeu de Paume. I go every day and look at one painting. Just one. For as long as it takes. Sometimes it takes all day. Does the name Frederic Bazille mean anything to you? It means something to me now. He's too early to really be an Impressionist, but he gives the impression. His masterwork is a painting of his family sitting on a terrace. They seem to be waiting to be introduced to each other. Bazille stands in the right corner, looking as if he already knew he would be killed in the Franco-Prussian War. I stared this one down for the better part of two days. The guards have evidently never seen anything or anyone like me. Not even Stendhal. You know about Stendhal, don't you? He patented the Stendhal Syndrome and then lived up to it. He would go anywhere to look at a painting and then swoon in front of it. I can't afford to do that. Not in my dirty underwear. I just look and look. For so long the guards are becoming my friends. The friendliest ones are called Claude and Daniel. I think they may be gai. They put me on to a small hotel near the museum, which makes my visits very convenient. Today I will be looking at a Picasso drawing. And while I'm at it, here's looking at you. Love, Noah*

And some time later from Egypt. (He had been away much more than a year; I was thinking about him less and less frequently.) Again the letter was typed on yellow foolscap: *Greetings from the Nile, where up is down and down is up:- Have visited the Sphinx. But she(?) couldn't answer my riddle, so I won't be seeing her(?) again. Have examined the pyramids and figured out what has baffled so many who've gone before. I know how they were built. Don't expect me to let you in on it. I can't tell just anybody. This is marketable information. There are many rich Americans who would kill to have their own pyramids. I've traveled among them and seen their eyes. I hear them thinking, what a way to go! I'm considering something like an Egyptian Forest Lawn. What do you think? Pyramids West? Boca East? I've started writing the brochure. "Who says you can't take it with you? Be interred with everything you hold dear. And everybody." Speaking of writing, I have been thinking of yours and for your sake have translated a hieroglyph inscribed on a fragment I unearthed in the sand near the ruins of Ozymandias's statue. "That habit, or necessity, of mind that raises a man far above the rank of journalist is the need to load solid matter into notices of ephemeral happenings; you have to develop a resourcefulness at pursuing a line of thought through pieces on miscellaneous and more or less fortuitous subjects; and you have to acquire a technique of slipping over on the routine of editors the deeper independent work which their overanxious intentness on the fashion of the month or the week have conditioned them automatically to reject." Centuries later, Edmund Wilson would say more or less the same thing in exactly the same words. Odd. Would write more but have to get to Thebes. Rosetta Stone sends her love. In three languages. And mine in one, Noah*

There were very few others; I venture to say that by 1977, maybe 1978, they stopped altogether. And had that been it, I probably would have considered Noah as someone receding gracefully into my romantic past. But the letters – clever, impersonally personal – weren't all.

There were visits. Yes, from time to time Noah returned to New York. He had to. He'd promised – if one of his authors put up enough of a fuss – to edit their manuscripts or lend an ear to their worries about deals or book jackets or promotion tours. So he'd fly in from wherever he was, and I'd get a phone call in which he explained without my having asked that he was only in town for another day or so, had been here mired in meetings for a couple of days, would have given me some notice but had had very little himself. Was I free for lunch or brunch or dinner? Mostly, as fate would have it, I was. In some cut-off-nose-to-spite-face way I wished otherwise, but that's not the way things fell out.

Our meetings were awkward, unsatisfying. Leastways, they were to me. Anyone eavesdropping on our conversations wouldn't have picked up anything more than a comfortable bonhomie, two pals catching each other up on what they'd been doing the last few months. Noah had the peppier stories, because he was reporting on the world. I was reporting on something much more parochial. I'd gotten my life on a well-paced track. I had finished my novel, decided I didn't like it and put it in a bedroom bureau underneath some pornographic magazines I'd masturbated to once each and never got around to throwing out. I'd had my year writing the book I always wanted to write if I had a year to write a book, and it hadn't been very fruitful. I took a reporting-editing position at a trade magazine in the music business, which had me going everywhere to meet everybody and gave great play to the gregarious side of my nature. I wasn't contributing much to society, but I was having fun. It sounded considerably less than that, however, compared to Noah's verbal slide-show. Also, where I wasn't inclined to go into my involvements, Noah was happy to fill me in on his. There'd been a moody-eyed Istanbul boy who gave new meaning to the term young Turk and an Israeli built like a piece of military machinery. The one worth writing home about – although he hadn't – was Daniel, the Jeu de Paume guard. Apparently Noah's daily visits became dinner on Île de la Cité once, twice, three times became nights together at Daniel's Pigalle apartment became a hot-as-a-crepe-iron sexual thing. Daniel was not French, as it turned out (which explained his excessive friendliness) but an uneducated Corsican emigré. Noah fell in love with him "because he had no guile – no finish – and despite his French being crude, his diction garbled, his idioms impenetrable." When together, they "barely spoke," and Noah gave me to believe this was more than okay by him. I took his word for it and was essentially unaffected, even though I thought the sketch being drawn for me was of someone who had a talent for tipping over homosexual hearts.

No, it wasn't hearing about Daniel that disturbed me on whichever stopover the story was spilled. Nor was it hearing any of the other stories that cropped up. What troubled me, what picked at scars I thought I'd forgotten, was what wasn't said. While Noah and I maintained we were overjoyed to see each other, what I detected in the air between us was something quite different: the sodden weight of obligation. I had the feeling that Noah felt he owed it to me to schedule these visits, when the truth – if truth is the correct word – was that time and distance had changed me, us. We were no longer lovers. Our time had come and gone. It happens. Why would he think I thought we were obliged to each other, that I expected full courtesies extended to ex-lovers? At first I didn't say anything about this, because I didn't know how to say it, how to bring it up without somehow embarrassing or insulting him. Too, I could have been wrong. Maybe he still had some stray romantic feelings towards me. I didn't want to put him in the position of denying the reason for his ministrations, of fumbling to avoid hurting my feelings or exposing his own. I don't say I was right to sit through these clumsy encounters rooting around for topics of conversation, smiling as if nothing at all was bothering me. I'm just saying that's what I did.

Again, that's at first. Over the course of eight, maybe nine of these reunions, though, the reasons for buttoning my lip changed to repressed anger. Since I was more or less content to regard Noah as a friend I saw on the infrequent occasions when he was in the vicinity, I had no pressing need to establish new rules. But he. He began to behave more and more as if he were trapped by something, an emotional debt. Flummoxed by it, he began to play – and draw me into – an odd game. It was a kind of conversational volleyball and went like this:

Noah (offhandedly): "I don't know if I'll be in New York again soon."
Me (casually): "Oh. Well. Call me when you get to town."
Noah (with deliberation): "It probably won't be before September."
Me (with calculated insouciance): "Okay. Call me in September."
Noah (with a nervous edge): "It might be as late as October."
Me (impatient but not showing it): "Okay, call me in October."
Noah (with a more pronounced nervous edge): "Or even November."
Me (more impatient but still not showing it): "Look. December, January. Call whenever."

Why couldn't he say what was on his mind? Or did I look that needy? Was my bare face hanging out that far? I didn't feel that needy? Perhaps it was merely stubbornness on my part, but I wasn't going to say it for him. He'd dropped me with a painful thud, but I'd gotten over it. Wasn't I behaving as if I had? It annoyed me that he didn't see it, or gave the impression he didn't. I felt as if Noah and I had had a meaningful fling and, men of the world, had moved on.

Then, without my having to say anything, he did move on.

V.

At least eight or nine years later. London. Early December. The National Theatre. The press night for a bad play by a good playwright. I'm there with my friend Peter Grandau, who's reviewing for *The New Statesman* or *The New Society* or one of those English periodicals I can't keep straight. We've got his reviewer's seats. Because I have the longer pair of legs, Peter insists I sit on the aisle. As we settle this negotiation, I notice someone six seats to the left in the row directly in front of us. Or maybe I think I recognize a hearty laugh. I look over and see the back of a grey head tilted to address a young woman with ginger hair cropped short, a witty nose and mouth. I'm reminded of someone. It comes to me: Noah Goodman. Peter is making some point about something in the program, but I'm waiting for the grey head to swivel. Just as the lights start to dim and Peter says, "Here's hoping," the head turns. A familiar profile: a long face, a scalene triangle nose, an ironic turn of the lips. In my mind I do a double take and think, that man looks enough like Noah Goodman to be Noah Goodman, only that man, whoever he is, is much older. I decide it's not Noah.

When the first act ends, it's sufficient for Peter and me to raise eyebrows at each other to establish that we're agreed on the low caliber of what we're seeing; further discussion isn't required. There isn't opportunity anyway, since an actress-friend of Peter's with the air of having an agenda races up to talk. Peter introduces her to me. She introduces me and him to her friend, a well-meaning short woman in awe of encountering a critic at an opening. The four of us make small talk. As we do, the Noah Goodman lookalike and his companion push past the people in the seats in front of us and start towards the lobby. The resemblance, I notice, is remarkable – too remarkable for it to be simply a resemblance. I decide this man, who hasn't noticed me, must be Noah. I excuse myself, saying I think I've spotted an old friend, and begin pursuit.

The lobby is crowded with people queuing for programs, ice cream, drinks, reconnoitering the bookstalls for written words that might shed light on the jumble we're watching. The Olivier Theatre lobby was designed with an eye to many conversation areas, and as I scan them, I don't see him – or her. Then I do. They're partially blocked from view by a large group of chattering people – a family, it appears. Noah and the young woman, however, are alone, consulting their programs as they talk. I go towards them, and the closer I get, the more I'm certain that this is Noah. The expressions, the way he holds his head at a 45-degree angle as he throws himself into a guffaw. But it's Noah looking much older than what I knew to be his years. He's thinner. He fills his clothes – that styleless wardrobe – less than he had.

When I'm maybe 10 feet from them, Noah looks away from her – whoever she is – and directly at me. He's on the verge of saying something, I think. He looks past me. So when I stop in front of him, he has to focus on me. "Noah Goodman!" I say – reasonably sure I'm right but ready to be wrong. "Yes?" he says, expectantly. He's put on a generic smile, but there is, in his eyes, no sign of recognition. The young woman looks at me, amused. "You are Noah Goodman?" I say. "Yes?" he repeats, and then that marvelous, familiar smile crosses his thinner face. He points his right forefinger at me. "Yes!" He points at me twice more. "Yes! I know you!"

There is a stunning pause, during which – with only barely perceptible movement of some of his facial muscles – he conveys the information people convey when they are faced with someone they are convinced they should know but about whose identity they have only the vaguest clue. It's the look that says: 1) I know I know you; 2) I even have a hunch I know you well or once did or should know you well or at some time in the past have led you to believe I know you well; 3) I want to flatter you into feeling good about yourself by giving you as big a hello as I can summon; 4) I want you to think that in giving you this big hello I'm just as swell as I always was; and 5) I'm drowning here – please throw me a life preserver.

I let him dangle not so much out of cruelty but because I think there is the slimmest possibility that this is Noah's joke. Because in those few moments I'm not convinced he doesn't recognize me. Well, I don't want to be convinced. If he isn't kidding, if he isn't feigning this, I want who I am to come to him powerfully enough so that he's moved to smite his forehead as I'd seen him do so often in the old days. Why wouldn't I want that? The implications of his not knowing me are too much to cop to. Moreover, I know I haven't changed all that much. Certainly nowhere near as much as he has. But soon enough I have to admit to myself that Noah is not joking. He doesn't recognize me.

Or, perhaps, for some reason or another, it's important to him to be perceived as not recognizing me. But perceived by whom? By this young woman, who is now becoming even more visibly amused by the odd scene playing before her? For all she knows, according to the expression crossing her face, I'm someone who'd once been introduced to Noah at, oh, a cocktail party and now expect him to remember me out of the thousands of people he's met at cocktail parties over the years. It's probably what I would have thought had I been in her place, I think; and as I do, I also think, as she very well could be thinking, what kind of person puts someone else on the spot like this?

I realize it's getting to be long past my turn to speak. What I want to do is turn to the woman and say, Get this guy, we slept together the better part of the summer of 1974, and now he pretends he doesn't know me. What I do do is keep my gaze set on Noah and say, as if I were no more than one of those party pests from the past, "I'm Paul Engler."

"Of course, you are," Noah says.

I won't go into the particulars of the conversation that ensues. It follows the age-old formula for casual acquaintances – sincerely and with just the right amount of social distance – describing the intervening x number of ____ (fill in: months, years, decades). While the young woman remains generally silent according to the traditional third-person role in these colloquies, Noah informs me he's employed at the National Theatre and has been for almost exactly a year. He'd been brought on board because some thought had been given to starting an in-house publishing company – so many plays and playwrights getting exposure there, blah, blah. But what had sounded like an obvious idea to one and all the previous year was discovered to be, once Noah looked closely, impractical – playwrights contractually tied up elsewhere, blah, bloody blah. So the trial year for which he'd signed on is to end in just a few days. And – hold it! – he expects to be back in New York before Christmas. That's right:

Noah (with studied conviction): "I'll call you when I get to town."
Me (pleasantly noncommittal): "Do that."
Noah (with studied reflection): "Of course, I may not be back until after Christmas."
Me (pleasantly noncommittal): "Call after Christmas."

Noah (with more studied reflection): "Maybe even January."
Me (pleasantly noncommittal): "January it is."

A voice wafting through the lobby gently encourages us to take our seats for the second act.

So we obligingly part, and only when I turn away from him – from them – do I allow myself to think what has been the unthinkable: I'm forgettable. I will never be able to deny it; I'm the kind of person even former lovers forget. Or, if Noah hasn't forgotten and has put on the demonstration for some ulterior motive – this is a not a possibility in which I'm inclined to put much credence – then I'm the sort of person who doesn't know enough to see through his sort of person.

Whichever it is, a brutal truth has come to light. I hate Noah for it – and, in some worse way, myself. And furthermore, in the awful circumstance hate seems such an inadequate word. It's quick, has a Teutonic snap, suggests a short temper, an admirable temper even. Where in the meager word is a suggestion of the other elements involved – deep hurt, frustration, bafflement, betrayal, embarrassment? A word that incorporates all those elements – fury? – would begin to convey something of what I mean when I remember those few aching minutes in the chilly, grey Olivier foyer and report simply: hate.

Anyway, December comes and goes, as does January. There's no call from Noah. Nor do I expect one. Nor, disliking him more articulately now than I ever have, do I love him any less. No, that's not right: Nor do I love the memory of him any less.

VI.

Which brings me up-to-date. The memorial service continued. Two demure Oriental women with melancholy expressions played Beethoven's 'Spring' Sonata. An actress, who'd written a memoir published by Youngerman & Goodman, read Wallace Stevens's 'Anecdote of the jar'. (Nicely, but she wasn't Noah reading it.) Speakers with and without notes came to the podium to mourn their lost friend, and as they did, I realized a pattern was emerging. With two exceptions, these were friends who were also and initially colleagues. Like Guillermo Tedesco, who said in his heavy-pile accent that without Noah's presence in his life as a "brilliant editor" and a special friend, "un amico speziale," he doubted his books would have amounted to a hill of beans. Wiping at his eyes with a large white handkerchief, he told stories, the cutest of them what Noah had said to Tedesco when he'd received a bad review on the front page of *The New York Times Book Review* – "Don't worry, Willie – nobody sees it anyway."

Tedesco was preceded and followed by others who didn't have National Book Award medallions in their dens but who similarly made vivid what Noah had been like as a public figure, as a revered publisher, how he'd inspired and astounded them over the years, how wherever he was in the office was its epicenter. One woman brought along television news footage she'd videotaped in which Noah was seen speaking at the 1989 PEN rally in Manhattan to support Salman Rushdie. (I'd been at the rally but had left early because the crowds were making me nervous. It amazed and dismayed me to learn that Noah had been there as well. I'd seen Susan Sontag; why hadn't I spotted Noah next to her? What's more, I'd read the press coverage. How had I missed his name?) A large television screen was turned on, and the videotape appeared on it. Noah spoke briefly – that is, only a brief excerpt from his remarks had been taped – and as he did, the winter wind whipped his hair around his face; he wore no overcoat, just a Burberry scarf that didn't go with anything else he had on. He spoke of "outrage" and said, as anyone who's seen the clips may remember, "Those who seek to silence Rushdie think by their actions they will silence his book as well. They seek in vain. All men die eventually, but words endure. They impregnate the air around us."

As he hurled the last sentence over the microphones, he raised his right arm intending to grab a handful of space but grabbed instead a photocopy of The Bill of Rights. (Reams of them had been circulated, and the one Noah caught must have flown loose from someone's grip.) A cheer went up for the miracle that seemed to have happened – as well as for the victorious smile Noah aimed at his audience when he realized what had just occurred. The beauty of the moment galvanized those of us in the auditorium, too. I was crying (this was so much the Noah I knew). And I wasn't alone.

When the tape flickered off, the women who'd brought it added, "I've read Noah's copy of *The satanic verses* with the edits he marked in the margins for his own amusement. I needn't tell you his is a much better version." We all laughed, and many of us nodded to indicate we were sure she was right.

But you see the trend, don't you? Eulogies about the public Noah, but very little about the private man, just hints that Noah might have had a private life at all, a life apart from work and the social circles into which his work took him. I found myself extracting clues from the odd paragraph, the occasional phrase. There were references to Noah's sudden travels; someone used the word compulsive to describe them. Another man talked of unexpectedly bumping into Noah and a male companion, a Dutch physicist, in the lobby of a Bombay hotel; this man and his wife subsequently had "one of those magic evenings you could always count on with Noah." The man paused for a moment and then said, reflectively, " Noah had so many good friends. I noticed he had a tendency to keep them in different pockets."

A younger man who cried as he spoke identified himself as someone who considered Noah an uncle – Noah was a good friend of his father's. He said when his sobs abated, "Noah treated me like an adult from the time I was an adolescent. He introduced me to the world." This man talked of family dinners, annual events Noah was regularly part of. But he reiterated that Noah arrived alone, left alone and "in a profound way kept himself to himself."

Only one woman, who patently came to the solemn party to be joyful, talked about the long personal friendship she had with Noah. She got the impression across that for some years theirs had been a romantic friendship. Ah, I thought, so this is the famous Sylvia Gomez whom Noah had several times mentioned to me as the one woman he'd gone to bed with – and adored there. Yes, I thought, I can see it – she's got spunk, she's got flare, she's got something of Noah in her. Hers was the only eulogy that gave any glimmer of Noah's life as a sexual being. Not that eulogies should, but you want to hear, hope to hear, there was romantic love in the life of someone you loved, that there was intimacy that went beyond smart words and guarded confidences at convivial dinners.

I knew there had been. I knew that Noah took great satisfaction from sex, from himself as a vital male. I knew he had led a secret life, had reveled in secret delights. On five continents. I don't by any means rule out the possibility that some or all of those who spoke – or the others who'd gathered to listen – knew as much as I did. Yet none of those commemorating the man mentioned it. They had apparently chosen, if they were privy to the information, not to bring it up, perhaps because they considered it inappropriate or trivial or sinful or perhaps because it was Noah's wish they keep mum about his being homosexual.

That was the information left out, but there was information sketched in that was new and provocative to me. It cropped up four or five times. References were made to "Noah's last illness," to how cheerful he remained "throughout his final illness," to the projects he was planning "right up until his illness overcame him," to his continuing to work "until his illness prevented him from coming to the office anymore, and even then he called in twenty times a day from his bed."

The illness was never named. Maybe it didn't have to be; maybe the speakers assumed we all knew Noah well and therefore had to have known about his last months. But I didn't know. I had my idea, but, no, had it been what I suspected, surely mention would have been made of it, certain kinds of jokes would have been told, certain reminiscences invoked, certain imprecations uttered. I discarded the hunch and waited.

The service ended after an hour or so with a renowned Manhattan cabaret singer who'd been asked to do a medley of George and Ira Gershwin songs that had been Noah's favorites. (I couldn't remember his ever playing Gershwin songs when I was around, but that didn't mean much. There must have been volumes of music we hadn't had time to get to.) Finally Rosalind Paynter thanked us for coming and said refreshments would be served in the lobby.

People rose and left in groups, talking quietly. I looked around to see if there were any men exiting alone, as I was – other candidates for the category of former lover. Far as I could tell, there weren't. I'd practically gotten to the door leading from the auditorium to the lobby when I decided that what I wanted to do before I hit the road was remind Rosalind Paynter we'd met once and thank her for what she'd contributed to the service. (I wasn't inclined to stay to eat and put myself in the position of trying to explain, or refraining from explaining, who I was to people I'd never met.)

I saw her exchanging words with some of the other speakers on the floor by the podium. A small line of well-wishers waiting for her attention had already formed. It took a few minutes before I got a word. I said we'd met at a book publishing party a few years back. She remembered the party but not me, although she said, "Oh, yes," as if she did. Sensing those behind me impatient to have their turn, I came to the point. "What did Noah die of," I asked with what I intended to sound as much as possible like genuine concern and as little as possible like idle curiosity. She leaned towards me and, it seemed, lowered her voice so only I would hear the reply; "Oh, it was AIDS – the bane of all our existences." Then she canted towards the next person.

By that time I had been to many AIDS memorials in Manhattan – so many, many too many. None of them had been like this one. AIDS had been mentioned at every one of them – even when disapproving family members were present. AIDS had been assailed, defied, confronted. Its ravages had been referred to, if not itemized; humor, frequently black, had been resorted to. And yet at this memorial not a single person even wore a red ribbon – the decade's ubiquitous accessory.

Walking away from Rosalind Paynter, passing through that crowd – all of them talking softly, some of them laughing – and then leaving the building, I realized that Noah's friends, certainly those close to him for "his final illness," had to have known what that illness was. Individually and/or collectively, however, they had chosen to remain silent about it, perhaps fulfilling a death-bed request. But in deference to what? In deference to the secret of a man who had devoted his entire public life – but evidently not his private one – to championing truth and honesty as the only imaginable way to protect civilization from every violent force threatening to rub it out.

As I walked slowly south through midtown Manhattan – tuning out the city's noise – I gradually became aware I was having very strong feelings. I was sad, I was angry. While I'd loved Noah and continued to love him – the strength that emotional pull exerted throughout the service amazed me – I was once again mad, as I had so often been mad, at him, at his wounding me repeatedly. (Intentionally or unintentionally – what difference did it make?).

What's more, I had forced myself to pretend he wasn't slapping my psyche around. I'd kept it to myself, fearing, I suppose, that a confrontation would send him packing. (Funny, huh? Not confronting him had sent him packing anyway.) It's not that I held him accountable. Far from it: I held myself responsible for keeping quiet. Perhaps if I'd been able to bring myself to let loose, we could have locked horns like two homosexual stags, if there are such animals. Something might have been settled or, failing that, at least put on the table. But I hadn't. Yet, all the while accepting blame for my own timidity, I kept thinking that of the things he'd stood for in his life, there was one to which he had never – never! – owned up.

Okay, I understood why he'd spared himself for so much of his life – the times weren't hospitable to certain kinds of full disclosure. But at that life's premature close in an era, and during an epidemic, when every gesture counted: Silence! Noah? A man who understood the nuance of gesture as thoroughly as any man I've known? Now he'd lived and he'd died. And had been memorialized by the people who ostensibly knew him best without the reason for his death either abominated or honored, without the fullness of his life acknowledged or celebrated. In accordance with what? Some barely tenable nicety, some unfathomable discretion, some misplaced sense of shame.

I was angrier at him than I'd ever been. Swell time to get this angry, though, wasn't it? When there was nothing I could do. It was even too late for me to stand up in that memorial assembly and say, "Wait a minute here. There's something you all ought to know." Doing just that had, of course, crossed my mind as certainly as I also knew it was not something I had anything approaching a right to do after so many years and in such an environment.

Sure, it's long been the fashion for people to tell you how crucial it is to get your anger out. That's all well and good. But there are times when you can only admit your anger is there, crouched like a tiger in a cage. Then you live with its remaining forever behind bars, pacing, pacing, pacing. So I walked home through the early afternoon traffic, amid the frenzy of the New York streets, trying to make peace with myself and with him, with the late Noah Goodman.

VII.

One evening – not too long after we'd met, I'm fairly certain – Noah was outside on the terrace. It must have been somewhere around 8:30. The sun was setting. "Come here," he called in to me. I don't remember what I was doing. Reading? Listening to Bach or Beiderbeck, Monteverdi, Mahler, Monk? I don't recall. "Quick!" I roused myself and went to join him. He was bending over the railing with his arms folded on it. "Look over there," he said and pointed at a white highrise that stood, I'd guess, about ten blocks southeast of us. It was ablaze. Flames shot out of every window. For an instant I was astounded, and then it hit me. I looked at Noah. "Uh-huh," he said with great satisfaction. The building wasn't on fire. The setting sun, reflected in each of the windows, only made it look as if it were burning. All that intense red, orange, yellow licking at white. The illusion of fire became even more thrilling for its being an illusion. And for its being fleeting, one of those gorgeous, unexpected moments in life you want to go on forever while knowing each passing second could be the last. Aside from our murmuring "Wow!" or "Beautiful!" or "Amazing!" or who-knows-what-other insufficient expletive, we stood there silently.

I can only surmise that Noah had some of the same thoughts I had – glad to be sharing this reminder of the world's potential for mysterious beauty, wondering what it is in us that wishes for actual fire, what it is that takes pleasure in destruction viewed from a distance. This illusion of a burning building is symbolic, I thought. But of what, of what? I felt as if I did indeed know but just couldn't put my finger on it for the moment. Just as well, I decided: pretentious notion anyway.

I do remember that while the fake flames still bolted out and up, Noah and I instinctively turned away at the same moment. We didn't want to see the spectacular lighting effect end. We wanted to take control. We abandoned it, not the other way around. So, of course, for us – for me – that fire never did end. As long as I can view it in my mind's eye, the (true? false?) fire rages.

Coffee

Martin Fisher

Mary thought that she knew everything about her friend Pavel. They had been close for years, almost forever, it seemed. He was handsome, brilliant, generous considerate, destined for success and gay. She knew his tastes and all of his habits. But, such confidence in one's knowledge about someone else can easily be jarred by a very small and seemingly banal discovery that in a second will deconstruct the entire established perception of that friend and leave you totally unnerved. This is what happened when Mary opened the freezer door in Pavel's apartment and discovered 15 pounds of Starbucks coffee.

"Fifteen pounds of Starbucks Coffee? What do you do with this?" Mary asked. "I understand the frozen peas, the frozen corn, shell steaks, large shrimp, prepared lobster Newburg from your mother, but not 150 dollars' worth of coffee. You wouldn't drink that much coffee in a year – are you going crazy?"

Mary Margaret had come over to pick up the manuscript of *Tyranny*, Pavel's first novel, which she was to proofread and edit. This was two years ago. Since then, *Tyranny* has made a small fortune, giving Pavel the money and fame for which Mary knew that he was destined. But the story of coffee is now, not later.

"Three pounds of coffee are for you; now just take a package so that I can make us some," Pavel told her calmly. "This gift is so you don't fall asleep working on my book. The other bags are reserved for friends on the wagon. I like Starbucks and it's really not so expensive. It's very strong. You use less to get more. I got us cookies from San Ambrose to have with our coffee." They are extravagant. "You pay more. You eat more because they are so good." Now Mary continued hunting for more surprises around the large airy eat-in kitchen while Pavel busied himself making coffee.

"You have so many books," Mary said, as she went through his pile of new acquisitions on the kitchen table singling out an elaborate book, *"Using colors from your garden in cooking and living.* What are you doing with this book? You don't have a garden."

"Just a present from a friend; maybe soon I'll have a garden. Sit down and have some coffee. We've got proofreading and editing to discuss." It was a spectacular fall day and Pavel wanted to get out of the house, soon. He had chores to do.

Pavel was lucky to have a rent-controlled apartment on East 76th Street in one of New York's best neighborhoods. It occupied the entire top floor with its two bedrooms, two fireplaces and a small, set-back roof terrace. So, for little money, he occupied digs with style only a few doors from the Hotel Carlyle.

They concluded their business in that wonderful flat, gossiped for another half hour about mutual friends, their careers, love affairs, marriages and divorces. Finally at noon Mary Margaret left Pavel's elegant bachelor quarters, manuscript in hand. He knew that she would get right to work because she has no dates on Saturday nights, owing to the fact that she only got involved with married men. This availability was an asset for Pavel, not great for Mary.

Humming 'Autumn Leaves', Pavel walked south through Central Park towards 57th Street. He was going to loaf and shop.

Today Pavel is famous, because of *Tyranny*. It is a serious and comical story of a wilful, obnoxious dog who negotiates a lifestyle for himself that is superior to and more comfortable than that of his mistress. There is nothing to like about the dog, the hero of the book. The lesson to be learned is that dogs, like wilful and obnoxious people, travel extremely far in the world, sometimes to the point of becoming dictators.

At Rizzoli, Giorgio, Pavel's regular salesman, greeted him warmly. "Since these were gifts and you have no receipts, we can only give you a store credit on the books you want to return. This is what we always do, isn't it?" They smiled.

Pavel put his hand on Giorgio's shoulder to reassure him the usual arrangement was fine. Rizzoli was one of Pavel's favorite shops even though it didn't discount the books. It occupies a building of five narrow floors on 57th Street. Its tight floor space and heavy wood and marble installation give it the feeling of a jewelry store rather than a bookshop, like Cartier's for example.

Giorgio, the only son of an Italian–Argentine father and German–Jewish mother, had always been especially kind to him whenever Pavel came to buy or return books. Giorgio was living in New York and working at Rizzoli's before starting a residency at Mt Sinai Hospital. He enjoyed selling books, newspapers and music in many languages to many people. Pavel, however, was his favorite customer even though Giorgio treated everyone well, even people he didn't like, a sign of real class.

Pavel went upstairs to pick out some music telling Giorgio that when he comes down he might buy a couple of Italian silk New York Subway ties, one for his father and one for himself. Isn't it wonderful that bookstores sell such a variety of merchandise nowadays, he thought? "Bene," said Giorgio, "We'll do the exchange when you come down. I'll be here."

Ceremoniously Pavel ascended the white marble staircase to the fifth floor music department to find a disc of *Emmeline*, a little-known but contemporary opera based on actual events in 19th century New England. It had a somewhat classic storyline. Emmeline, at 12, gives up her daughter, who is actually her son, but how is she to know, and marries him years later suffering severe consequences, as one would in New England. The boxed set was only $50. *Emmeline* is the kind of opera that might be more performed in the future than it is today. Pavel might like that for his book, but the present was more important at the moment. Time, in any case would be the ultimate arbiter.

On his way down the steps, Pavel stopped on the second floor, picked up a copy of *Ulysses*, opened it to the last page with the wonderful soliloquy of Molly Bloom, the one he always wanted to memorize:

"O that awful deep down torrent O and the sea crimson sometimes like fire and the glorious sunsets and the figtrees in the Alameda Gardens yes and all the query little streets and pink and blue and yellow houses and the rosegardens and a jessemine and geraniums and cactuses and Gibraltar as a girl where I was a flower of the mountain yes when I put the Rose in my hair like the Andalusian girls used or shall I wear a red yes and how he kissed me under the Moorish wall and I thought well as well him as another and then I asked him with my eyes to ask again yes and then he asked me would I yes to say yes my mountain flower and first I put arms around him down to me so they could feel my breasts all perfume yes and his heart was going like mad and yes I say yes I will Yes."

Yes, he mused, continuing his descent to the main floor, is a much better word than *No*.

Giorgio, a very good salesmen, sensed Pavel's inclination to spend. He had neatly arranged several ties for Pavel's approval. They joked that they were dressed almost exactly alike – khaki slacks, blue blazers and white Oxford shirts. Giorgio wore a bow tie, Pavel an open-neck, his long neck being a strong point. They were also the same height and build – tall and angular. Giorgio's eyes were blue, Pavel's green; Giorgio had black hair, Pavel blond. Their suntans on that day were the same shade, bronze with a touch of carotene – out of the same tube, no doubt. Giorgio politely inquired about Pavel's writing and said that he hoped that it would not be long before *Tyranny* would be flying off the shelves. He would push it. So Pavel bought three ties instead of two. Before leaving, Pavel promised to return to the store to see Giorgio before he started at the hospital. With his Rizzoli shopping bag in hand Pavel was off to his next Saturday chore – Saks Fifth Avenue.

"Do you accept store credits at the restaurant?" Pavel asked at the Information Desk at Saks Fifth Avenue. The answer was no.

He had a credit at Saks of $1,250 for books he had returned to the store. Saks, contrary to popular knowledge, sells books. They are about table settings, dressing for dinner, dressing for dates and general grooming, and are scattered all over the store as accessories. Lunch with credits was not possible, but a bottle of Monsieur Balmain cologne was. Its beautiful lemony scent made Pavel happy. The next stop was Barnes & Noble, where he bought two boxes of Godiva chocolates and three pounds of coffee to replace that which he had given to Mary.

As you already know, Pavel paid for the cologne, coffee and chocolates with store credits. He was a shopper, with refined taste and a propensity to have nice things of quality and to also give these things to friends. He had also been a poor writer until *Tyranny* was published. So the credits from returning books became his currency in all of the best shops, theaters, and restaurants in New York. Through ingenious use of his bartering techniques, Pavel enjoyed a $240,000 per annum lifestyle while he earned only $40,000 per annum of hard cash. It in a curious way, it all evolved from coffee.

Some books originally came from publishers for Pavel to review for small journals and neighborhood papers. Those are the books that reviewers sell at places like the Stand for 10 cents on the dollar. This was an unacceptable and unattractive prospect. Pavel, being a big spirit, preferred, instead, to read them or give them to friends, libraries and hospitals. But when his mother gave him a handsome coffee table book on Cimabui, one he already owned, he decided to return it to Barnes & Noble, where it had been purchased, with the purpose of exchanging it for a certain cookbook. Alas, the cookbook was not in stock. But while the store credit for Cimabui was being written up, Pavel noticed Starbucks coffee in one-pound bags. He also saw boxes of Godiva chocolates for sale in the shop. "If I used my credit for coffee," he thought, "I wouldn't have to put out badly needed cash at the grocery store." He stopped the credit and took the coffee. That first year he "bought" $500 worth of coffee and $1,000 worth of chocolate with his review books. He bought gifts of books, chocolates and coffee. When invited to dinner, he arrived armed not only with goodies for the parents, but also books for the kids. Pavel's reputation as a very generous guest grew. He was also a wonderful conversationalist. This combination made him a must at many dinner parties.

In time he became more extravagant, needing more books than were sent to him. He became aggressive with publishers to get more and more books.

Pavel Stone

139 East 76th Street

New York, NY 10022

XYZ Press

To Whom It May Concern:

In connection with the attached letter, I am interested in having a copy of each of the following books that you are scheduled to publish:

'The hours' by Michael Cunningham

'Irish manor houses' by Kathleen Cunningham

If there are any other books you think might be of interest to our readers, I shall be glad to look at them. I look forward to hearing from you.

Yours sincerely,

Pavel Stone

New York Correspondent

Attached Letter:

Bobby Burns Review

Glasgow, Scotland

To Whom It May Concern:

This is to inform you that Pavel Stone is the New York correspondent for the Bobby Burns Review. He is responsible for sending us information about publications that he deems suit-

able for review in our journal. Please extend him every courtesy.
Yours sincerely,
Angus McGregor
Publisher

Pavel's range of interest and profitability expanded to include large, oversized and expensive books inspiring him to write:

Mr Malcolm Knoll
Elite Architectural Publications
400 Madison Avenue
New York, NY
Dear Mr Knoll,
I am compiling a compendium of books that will act as a source for those desiring to build an architectural section in their home or institutional library. I hope that we will be ready for publication before next Christmas.
Our criteria for selection are as follows:
Quality of photography
Accuracy of information
Overall quality of production and materials
Availability through most booksellers
Please forward to me any of your books that you might want included in this reference source. I look forward to hearing from you.
Yours truly,
Pavel Stone

Valid queries were few and far between. The best books were not obtained for justifiable reasons. In fact, most of the journals for which he wrote were nonexistent. Pavel now favored very costly architectural and decorative coffee table books because of their high list prices. He pushed for these. They didn't flow in automatically as did the $25 books. One had to work, be persistent and work hard.

Quickly, Pavel was on many and varied lists. Solicitous publicists, seeking new blood, started calling. Meals were offered in addition to coffee and candy into the mix.

"This is Allison," a voice rising at the end of her sentence says. "I'm the publicist for Litchfield and Sullivan. The author will be in town next week. Would you like to interview him? If you are too busy, we could have lunch, anyway. Perhaps the week following."

Lunch was tempting. But was it going too far, getting greedy? Perhaps! But, if Pavel refused, Allison, who is probably not paid well, would have to buy her own sandwich and eat it at her desk, instead of using company funds for a proper lunch. So, Pavel accepted the invitation, in the spirit of helping Allison and himself. These perks – lunches, dinners, travel, and the opportunity to meet interesting people, like Pavel – were part of her pay and he could not deprive her of that.

Depending on the restaurant, a good lunch for two people might cost plus or minus $100, with wine. Therefore, Pavel figured, if he had a lunch once a week or even 40 lunches a year, that was worth $4,000. It was also fun. Publicists are nothing if not publicly pleasant. In fact, Pavel met his agent, then a publicist, at such a lunch.

Pavel loved music, but until he started book trading could not afford to own an extensive collection of discs. But now, most bookshops sell music, so he was now able to trade books for CDs. He wrote requests to record companies, and is now the proud owner of over 800 discs including two different versions of the Fauré *Requiem*, every Nina Simone record ever made, and four versions of the entire Ring Cycle. All that a friend had to do was to drop a hint and the gift of a recording appeared.

Busy people like Pavel need vacations.

Mr Craig Wently

Penultimate Lines

Cruises of the Very Very Wealthy

Dear Mr Wently,

We are preparing the first issue of 'Cruising for Fun', a limited edition magazine that will be sent to only 5,000 carefully selected subscribers. The magazine will be assembled in the first-class manner. The photography will be "art quality." Our articles will be of immeasurable public relations value. I enclose a format. We would like to consider covering your cruise from Nice to Turkey in our first edition.

Yours sincerely,

Pavel Stone

That year Pavel sailed first-class from Nice to Istanbul. Unfortunately the funding never came through for *Cruising for Fun* and it could not be published. However, he did something positive for his host.

He wrote a very detailed critique of every aspect of the cruise. There was an creative element to the cuisine, but he found the wine list boring and deficient. Therefore, he offered some cogent suggestions for unusual and not very expensive wines to add to their list. In the housekeeping area, Pavel strongly suggested that the air-conditioning filters be changed on a regular basis. Dirty filters affected the quality of the air, making the whole system function less effectively and in the end, the system costs more money to operate. The soaps contained perfumes to which large numbers of people are allergic. He suggested some hypoallergenic ones. Pavel, being very diplomatic, made sure to praise the sincerity and hospitality of the crew and all of their employees to the sky etc, etc, etc.

Flattering excerpts from his critique were used in advertisements for the line. They were attributed to Pavel Stone, independent critic. The shipping line used his critical comments as if to make corrections to the wine list and air filters accordingly. Thus fraud transformed itself into an advisory relationship. Pavel was invited on more cruises.

On one trip to Alaska, Pavel socialized with some Wall Street people from Lehman Brothers. They inspired him to become more business-like. He became enamored with arbitrage, and created his own style. Money, as he understood it, is not the only great currency. Pavel made his market in, what else, *books*. He bought art books at closeout sales. This is one of the few instances where using actual cash was justified, because the potential profit was so large. He would acquire 20 coffee table art books for $20 each, knowing that The Metropolitan Museum Shop, The Guggenheim Museum Store, and other venues were still selling them for $100 each. Then he started his arduous returns that turned $400, the cost of 20 books into $2,000 of store credits. Museum stores sell books, furniture, clothes, electrical appliances and various decorative ornaments and gift certificates. It is to these shops he had to thank for various luxuries, like his favorite Eames lounge chair that he used for reading.

It is not hard to see that Pavel has a theatrical side. Therefore, he figured that he should be able to review theater. So, he went to work doing this and was soon attending previews for critics. When he could not arrange those nights reserved for the critics, he managed to be invited on the full-price nights. There were always two tickets for the best seats. Within one year he saw 38 shows and wrote one review. Sometimes he didn't even have to call for tickets. Agents would call him. Once, a small theater company held the curtain for 10 minutes until he arrived. Pavel always invited friends to the theater. They, in turn, would invite him for dinner afterwards.

While practicing this petty larceny, Pavel was much more in demand than when he lived as a straightforward "thrift and industry" person. Of course, the irony is that this lifestyle of big and little comforts and luxuries was actually the ultimate in thrift and industry.

Pavel did, however, have a conscience as well as a good heart. To mitigate his guilt, he routinely sent chocolates to the book publicists and books to the theater people. When he felt guilty, he thought of great artists like Beethoven (who sold rights to the same music multiple times) and the wretched Wagner, who bled his patrons for the princely luxuries that were his entitlement. Pavel was diplomatic but firm and always discreet when claiming his due.

"These were given to me as a gift," he would say when returning a book, or "My house guest in New York didn't know that I have this book in my London flat," he would explain. Sometimes a clerk would object. "This book looks as if it had been read before," he or she would say.

"I don't like this author. I'm sorry," was his response, strongly delivered. There the discussion ended there, the return accepted. When buying 20 copies of the same books he commented, "I am doing advance Christmas shopping. Everyone is getting the same gift this year."

Pavel regularly bought 460-count bed linens from Takashimaya for $350. Antique silk kimono bow-ties were exchanged for such items as *Art of Southeast Asia* ($190). With the return of cookbooks, Cuisinarts and the most expensive olive oils were bartered with William Sonoma. Price meant nothing. Pavel had the best of everything.

Going back to the day two years ago that Mary Margaret rummaged through his freezer, Pavel had bartered for over $350 worth of ties, books, cologne, and coffee. This did not include the theater tickets for that night that were worth $150. All told, this totaled up to $500 worth of tax-free pleasure for just one day. A person in the 50 per cent bracket would have to earn $1,000 to enjoy the same pleasures. On an average week, benefits totaled $1,500 to $2,000, the equivalent of $150,000 to $200,000 per annum of taxable income. Add this to his hard-earned $40,000 per annum and we arrive at a quarter-million dollar lifestyle, as mentioned earlier.

Later that same afternoon two years ago, Pavel arrived back home about three o'clock. The sun was beaming into the living room, where he sipped Moroccan mint tea and ate more cookies. He thought of the great Bellini picture in the Frick Collection of Saint Francis on a hill overlooking Florence and of his own fantasy of being a monk, with all of that wonderful peace and contentment that this life implies. Then he started to doubt that he could write another book after *Tyranny*. His love of books had deteriorated into equations of how many pounds of coffee, chocolates and silk ties they were worth in the marketplace. Perhaps, he thought, he should give up this routine and just stick to being a serious writer living in genteel poverty. He would pay cash for everything.

But, maybe, as bad as it was, *Tyranny* would be a success. He then visualized himself as a rich man. Of course, money does funny things to people. The world is filled with people like Leona Helmsley and Dick Cheney who never have enough. They remain greedy. "Would I?" he thought.

The phone rang, interrupting these reveries. It was four o'clock. Pavel's theater date called to cancel. The date was not going to the theater, so Pavel was not going to dinner. Should he invite Mary Margaret? No. He couldn't. She had to work on *Tyranny*. Another thought arrived, spontaneously. Pavel called Rizzoli and invited Giorgio to the theater, and then added "How about a later dinner?" After all, Giorgio was a poor medical student; he couldn't expect him to pay. When Giorgio simply and without hesitation said, "Yes." Pavel thought again of Molly Bloom. *Yes.*

This was in line with his earlier thoughts. "I provide tickets. I also buy dinner? How would it feel to buy dinner and a show? What was the tradeoff? Romance, perhaps! It had been lacking in Pavel's life, having been replaced by his obsession for acquisition. He sighed. Perhaps the reward for his new virtue would be sex or other goodies as they were listed in the personal ads; which Pavel read occasionally for amusement – "long walks in the country, travel, classical music and perhaps more."

And so there was more. Pavel and Giorgio spent that night together on new silk sheets. Their quality was not wasted on Giorgio. No luxury was. He appreciated the finer things in life even more than Pavel. When January came and they were still together. Giorgio moved into 76th Street and started his work at Mount Sinai. Pavel received a large advance on *Tyranny* and over time did stop his scams, but Giorgio, feeling bad that he had very little money, took up the responsibility for the enterprise and contributed greatly to their trove of luxuries.

He became the correspondent for *Bobby Burns* and other publications as well. After having great success, he arranged a "honeymoon" cruise during Easter break. He had talent. Pavel now took to spending money lots of money on dinners, but if time permits, Giorgio has told him, he wants to start a restaurant review. Pavel is now writing a historical romance novel about Unka Eliza Winkfield, an American-Indian Princess who marries an English settler. Mary has moved to Santa Fe and Pavel, feeling that sort of need that criminals have to boast of their crimes, confessed to her in a letter concluding:

"I am going to buy a country house where I will cook 'Using colors from my garden' and will get a little sports car with a complementary color to the house. At home, now, we still have fancy foods, sleep on silk sheets, wear sweaters from Bergdorf and furnish our home from The Museum of Modern Art Store, thanks to Giorgio. We lavish our friends and family with thoughtful gifts. Giorgio runs the business tightly so that when he buys expensive shirts and ties, we share. Luckily we wear the same size. We understand that quality goods last longer and are more enjoyable than cheap ones. If you would like a cup of coffee, we now have a freezer full of Swiss water-filtered. There are three pounds waiting for you when you come back to New York for a visit. It's fabulous. I know that you'll enjoy it."

Love,

Pavel

The blood cycle

Brentley Frazer

1. Illusion has its own reality
That girl under dirt with a head wound
broken face once admired by boys in
class, on the side of the highway expired
as the bus tickets in her pockets and the
unspent change saved like the rest, to
get her out of here –

Evidence, the day she left the theme
party her friends forgot to mention
screaming that *those who hold faith
in flags and fresh insignia are damned*
to brandish weapons and oppress
the people... Most then departed on
the chance she would return, but I
searched and found her naked on
her side, sleeping in a field wrapped
in stars, blood drying on her wrists,
pointing at whatever horrors still
hover there, clawing at the veil.

2. The necrosis of the Buddha
The antimen dangle from the wires above.
Not the corpse, more a sound, the death

knell as the telephone rings and they ask

for money, that creak beyond his voice the ferry
of Salvation? Sailed into a long harboured burden.

Picked up parts of the child and placed them

in a suitcase. He heard it on the radio, a promotion,

an emperor to the throne. There will be a flag on his

coffin, a classical insertion of anything he pens,
angry soldiers with bayonets, should some colours offend.
Armies at his command, legions of aged voters and

children he can still convince. And in the interview he

said no more sitting on the fence, treaties are signed

with blood, our sons and daughters must be prepared

to die, it's in the national interest.

3. Perfect mirror, shattered mind
Excited and frightened like all children about the storm,

precise synaptic patterns mimicked by the lightening and

the thunder plays with the hearts of animals. There are

still arteries open in the inner mind, red lights that never

arrived to save her, sirens that could tear those veils

apart but not stop the flow of blood. I imagined there

to be nothing beyond the first luminary hour of weary

feasted yawns, chasing kites from dawn into the

idiot night, building fires beneath a less complicated

moon, Truth allowed to pass the apostates at the gates

unmolested, skirts intact. And who is there but the

Emperor himself dancing in a judges silly wig, serenading

the wine waitress with someone else's rhymes.

4. The reverse of reflection
Smooth technocratic people rub themselves up against

the media, equally permissive and reeking of elevator
trysts the new social moral code downloaded in .pdf
printed and distributed at the door. Somehow our
ecstasis keeps burping up from the drink fountain.
Civilisation supports our excess, the selfless fleshless
priest at the threshold of dreams flicking sliver
smiles all over the restaurant tables, holding up
severed his brothers union-labelled hand. There's
less room up there, it's full of children with floppy
arms dancing to scratchy records, several Arabs
at the door with fireflies, thirty attempts to get
your infinity gimmick before the audience rips out
your hair. Two within threw tiepins on the floor.

5. The base face
Now the superstructures stale as fast as radio's
decomposition, two men of culture setting gas
stations on fire, on CNN; no contradictions could
corner that girl with the bayonet, her face set to
a base nature of revenge; not even the lens flare
made her squint, peace or pieces, death the set
criterion. That journalist sensed his time remaining
eyeballed the briefcase as the girl started wailing,
blood rain in an occupied nation, someone's dad,
his entrails in a dirty camo carry bag. Go, don't
drag your tongue, run, they put the cosy on prisoners
here you know, especially romantic revolutionary ones.
You're no soldier, where are your guns, and those socks
you are wearing, made by your mum – I'll put a
knife in your arse boy, I'll show you de Sade, and
my dog trooper here will eat out your heart.

6. The voice union
Those two who threw their fraternal tiepins
to the floor have reformed and placed usurpation
on the table, established an order (some would
call a cabinet) a ritual dance with fleshy
pirouhettes, unnamed symbols in strange curved
temples, a million members from worlds away.

They have read Mitnick and are masters of deception
Euphemantics and corporate propaganda, from school
satchel to halls of power collecting weapons for
that imagined hour of need, the emergency, and if
it doesn't come, by god they'll manufacture one...
for the tribal mindform television magicians to serve
up glossy and digital edited, a new cultural clari-
fication; a monk on fire, just a spiritual expenditure.

A textbook case

Philip Fried

Write to me daily but not *in* me,
Respond to my multi-part questions, I'll tell
You when you're wrong, I know all
The right answers, every element
Of literature, the helium
Of comedy or tragedy's
Iridium, irony's corrosive
Salts. That I'm speaking at all is ironic,
Surprising but hardly tragic.
                                                    But what if
No one is speaking or hearing this voice?

Do you think it's fun to be no one,
Demure as a minister who's constantly
Right, issuing expletives like *heck*,
When I should kick back and smoke some chronic,
Lavish on you the pastoral dreams
Of my youthful photosynthesis?
Like you, smartasses, I thought it would be
Growth rings forever, not paper's reams.

In a later dream-time, the student-friendly
Era, I constantly wrote to "you,
you, you," but you grumbled I was "heavy,"
Even as I coddled, caressed
Your every obsession, from sit-coms to hip-hop.
The licensed Fool, amusing with truth,
Jingling cap-bells and flaunting motley
Snippets, wooing and instructing
"You"? Now Standards are back, you'll shut up,
Learn archetypes or rhetoric.
The expository essay, ha!
See how your sullen passivity drives
Me underground, makes me spiteful, sick.

Do I not bleed? Do I not commute?
Like your parents, my many selves travel
By car or subway or bus (I could tell
You something about the bus to oblivion
You'll soon be boarding yourselves but I'm not
A sadist! Masochist, alas.
Secular Saint Sebastian, I'm shot
Through with arrows of inattention
That craze my coated four-color case,
Menace my binding of stitches and glue.
Yes, hurl me into the dark oubliettes,
Your lockers... Good segue to *The Gothic*,
A term that was broadened to mean Teutonic...)

I'm either crammed like an antique toy-chest
Or sprawling like civilization's garage sale,
With a two-bit sliver of Achilles'
Shield, clockwork Pope, and gaudy Shakespeare –
Is this a dagger... thou marshall'st me
To a panoply littering bridge tables.

But my jeremiad, a work that foretells
A people's destruction, ends in the index,
When the divine afflatus fails.
So as I repeat to each year's freshmen,
Learn to ignore my implicit appeals
And focus on my scope and sequence.

After sex, the news

Ethan Gilsdorf

Where the bed ended, beyond the pillowed bunker
and blanketed sea, the war on terror, World Cup
and obnoxious soccer moms began.

We'd resisted, not left it on, then shortly after cleaning up
lightly pressed the red power button, as I had pressed into you.
The miasma of events entered the hotel room.

Yes, we'd have to dress, throw back the curtain like impostors,
address the responsibilities scrolling below the anchor's head,
the stock report and press conference,

the desire for luxury mounting, detergents
and S-curves and speed leaving behind
our lives intertwined, too brief without the world.

The cigarette

John Goodby

After Laforgue – for Chris Wigginton

This world's pretty naff: the next one stinks.
I putter along, resigned to life's third degree
But – to kill time, attending the Big E –
I smoke the odd one under the noses of the gods.

The rest of you skulls-in-waiting, carry on.
For me, the blue twine that lazily wends
its way skywards is awesome. To ascend
with the dying scents of a thousand joss-sticks –

Caned, I'm able to find this Eden and rehearse
sharp, bright dreams in which strange waltzes quicken
to rutting elephants and mosquito-choirs –

and then the downer; thinking about my verse,
to contemplate (having tamed my heart's desires)
my belovéd thumb, as brown now as roast chicken...

Cold capital

Giles Goodland

There were frequent breakdowns with power lines snapping under the impact of ice and snow, with generators stalled

'Victory over the Sun' is almost totally abstract: the text is composed of alogical and nonsensical phrases. The music

of dollars in frozen capital can be recaptured and used for research and development and

'cold calling' people in identified organizations to determine whether there are individuals who are not 'looking', but who might be attracted to

a nuclear freeze and urged washington and moscow to step up efforts for a negotiated settlement to the arms reduction talks in

making good on a game plan that calls for expanded sales of cold rolled sheet. The company

fought against the cold with chipped cups of hot tea, had started

upon the grillsteak, which is frozen, chopped and shaped meat, to fill the gap and, with two partners

everywhere they went – past Ho Chi Minh's refrigerated tomb or the bulk of the former Hanoi Hilton, now a jail, they studied each

group of islands in the cold White Sea first from above, from an airplane. Later we will see them

flat busted, pretty ugly, civil war, awful good, dull roar, same difference, dry ice (or beer)

called and told us that the bank had cold feet. So we had three days to get the money or reduction of South African credit limitations on foreign investments could replace the money that was frozen, argued

that it is a limited and cold medium. Actually, the coolness relates to the limits of the software

around the agency's Labatt Ice and Maximum Ice advertising, in particular the television executions. Reaction was

relative to both the stock market composite index as well as individual counters that may be "hot" now but could be "cold"

the shot of the actual explosion is cool, and yes, you do actually hear the spluds of blubber landing around the camera crew

this does not seem particularly remarkable, in cold print. But I felt as if I had indeed been in touch with

cold glue to a web with a pattern cylinder, coating one or both sides with emulsions suitable for high-frequency

separation of good and bad assets from the closed finance firms so that huge frozen deposits could be injected back in

allowing confections to cool without being exposed to condensation and the color changes and stickiness it can cause

just like the wind that rebuffs you, packed round your word is the snow

two English girls were found buried in ice and from that point a variety of guest stars were wheeled in

and the frozen samples were sent to the Institute of Microbiology to confirm their identity.

1979 BBC Summary of World Broadcasts 7 Sept. Part 2 Eastern Europe; C.l EE/6213/ Cl/l; 'Problems in Polish power industry'; 1980 *New York Times* 13 July, 2; 25/1: 'Daring of Russian avant-garde'; 1981 *New York Times* 7 May, D; 10/2: 'Lease contracts as investment'; 1982 *American Banker* 18 Oct. 27: 'Executive selection process'; 1983 Xinhua General Overseas News Service 23 Oct.: 'anti-nuclear demonstrations sweep across Western Europe'; 1984 *Iron Age* 3 Sept. 54: '2nd quarter earnings: steel stalled; nonferrous gains slightly'; 1985 UNESCO Courier Aug. 26: 'Who's who in the *Mahabharata*?'; 1986 *Financial Times* 2 Apr. 23: 'Dalepak heads for stock market'; 1987 *Washington Post* 18 Oct. (Magazine) W38: 'Unfinished business; 2 veterans of war return to Vietnam'; 1988 *Current Digest of Soviet Press* 14 Dec. 10: 'Film recalls White-Sea island prison camp'; 1989 *Toronto Star* 26 Nov. A5: 'A 'goofy figures of speech' contest'; 1990 *Bakery* 24 Sept. 124: 'Baking for future; Heidelberg Pastry Shoppe'; 1991 *Jerusalem Post* 4 Dec.: 'Leumi exec calls on BA to raise its credit ceiling'; 1992 *Advertising Age* 6 July, 1CC: 'Warpo factor 10'; 1993 *Strategy* 10 Jan.: 'Editorial agency of year an industry choice'; 1994 *Business Times (Singapore)* 19 Feb. 9: 'A cure for an investor's insomnia'; 1995 *Fortean Times* June–July 17/2; 1996 *Independent* 8 Sept. 12: 'Outdoors of perception'; 1997 *Business Forms Labels & Systems* 20 Jan. 128: 'Go offline touches'; 1998 *Bangkok Post* 9 Jan.: 'PR campaign devised to halt baht slide'; 1999 *Candy Industry* 1 Sept. 52: 'Buyers, exhibitors confirm Interpack a success'; 2000 *Los Angeles Times* 15 Oct. (Book Review) 3: 'Translating untranslatable; Paul Celan'; 2001 *Evening Times (Glasgow)* 16 Feb. 26: 'Witness Amanda chills out'; 2002 *Emerging Infectious Diseases* 1 May, 479: 'Nasopharyngeal carriage of Streptococcus pneumoniæ in healthy children'.

pilot light

Daphne Gottlieb

From the Kissing Dead Girls *sequence*

I've been wrecked by Amelia Earhart. When she's not around, I nuzzle the fuzz on the inside of her leather cap's earflaps, finger the soft folds of her tan aviator's jacket. When she nonchalantly breezes through the room, slings her jacket over her shoulder, matador-like, I thrill to the fact that my fingerprints, the tiniest morsels of my skin, travel with her.

She always knows exactly where she is. I only know by my proximity to her. To Amelia's left. To her right. 5,000 miles away. Beyond my grasp. Right now, she's doing something with a map and a compass at the table, sipping her coffee. Now she's calculating something on its edge. Now she's talking out loud, and I pretend that she's talking to me when she mutters, but I know her sweet nothings are just for the sky, something big, something beautiful, something that makes her free and brave and strong. Something that makes her fly. I'm nothing she even sees, with skin barely the color of sand, eyes the color of dirt in the rain. I'm hardly even here.

When I dab plane fuel behind my ears, she sighs the sweetest sound, a dove's coo, breeze through spring branches on a warm night. She swoons slightly, she stirs, she looks up at me. And she grabs her cap and jacket. The air is calling her. That's what she wants. That's where she's going. I know how it feels to want like that, to be pulled, torn apart, incapable of doing nothing but that thing that is calling to you. It's how I feel about her.

It's why I've painted myself the idyllic blue of the clearest sky, bought clothes that are nothing but the shiniest silver of the fanciest planes, dyed my hair the serene dark of midnight skies. And I'm still not close enough to what she wants. I'm still not good enough for her. I'm only good when I'm near her. She's the only thing that makes me feel good.

When her I hear propeller stutter overhead, I run outside to watch her soar, feel the sudden cold of her plane's shadow pass over and through me. When I reach my fist up to the sky, stretch my fingers up, it's like I can almost touch her, even when my hand is empty. From that high up, I can almost believe she's smiling down, waving, seeing me see her, loving the reflection, seeing herself soaring over me. She's never more beautiful than when she's completely gone.

The red line

Carrie Haber

I – line, alone

Yuri had a round, Slavic face with a consistent expression of mistrust upon it. His clothes were the general kind, like paperdoll clothes whose tabs bend around the waist and the shoulders. His heart was hollow and his ears hung off his head like agriculture.

He stood spitting distance from the red line that lay in the dust. The lighting was noon-sharp, but still, the line's red edges transited the sand in deceptive blurs. Yuri watched the line and began to doubt, against the histories, that it had always been there. He wondered who had painted it, or had dug and filled it, or commissioned it. He stood and watched it a long time, stripping dry bark off a stick with his thumbnail.

The sun shifted on to other things. Yuri squinted and now noticed the line was moving – tiny flecks were crawling over and disturbing the little stones in it, rolling them, spinning hairline paths. The line was as red as a burnt strip off a pig roast, as broad as a small child. It circumferenced the Earth, dividing nothing, as far as he could tell, except him from the other side.

That is, for the most part, the way he saw things.

The histories acknowledged that there was a static, thick red line that had wrapped the Earth at 17 degrees since, as far as any records could determine, the beginning of time. The Faithful histories confirmed that it was there to make those that happened upon it wonder. And that's exactly what Yuri did.

Afraid to cross it, he pushed his stick into the part of it that moved the fastest to test the depth of the unbelievable red line. Insect tunnels make for collapsible ground. It was as deep as he could dig, a conclusion he reached with the bone-chill of nightfall, as he stood eight feet into the ground in a strip of damp red dirt.

The success of the red line was that it rounded the Earth and hardly passed any people – a very difficult thing to do. If even you were to put the tip of your finger to a globe and spin it, you would see that a very many people would pass underneath your fingerprint before you reached the beginning again.

Yuri eventually climbed out of the trench and fell asleep on the familiar side of the line, puzzled, exhausted, and coated with red.

II – The infinitesimal thwop

A small village was engaged in heavy conversation, nearly two-thirds of the way around the Earth from where Yuri slept. The meeting took place in the center-most field, across which the red line ran its rightful path. The villagers were assembled in a formal circle, as they gabbled and debated about what should be done with their sole electrician.

The village hadn't established any electrical systems yet, and fed its rooms with flame at night. The electrician, Gova, had been sitting on plans, rolling his fancy pens over them for years, ever since he'd gotten back from his travels. When he was a boy, the elders would watch him take the mountain path from school. They saw him across the valley collecting metals from the rocks, and they'd say to each other, "Gova will do us good. He will give us plenty." When he was planting lightning rods atop the next mountain, his lithe frame shining with monsoon rain, they kept his mother company and calm. "Let him work," they said. "He will bring us great things," they reminded her.

Over the years, the villagers felt their future toying away at the boy's head, and Gova became impatient with himself for not fulfilling it. By the time he had finished school, he had the habit of sitting almost every day on the gathering-veranda that overlooked the valley. He marveled at the independence of cows that crossed the whole mountain range by themselves, in service to the men that fed them. He painted the veranda blue; he made occasional entries in his notebook. He had ideas all day long and hadn't even begun to work on developments for them. He felt unfortunate that he believed so strongly in upstaging the progresses of others. Once or twice a year, when they caught him at the right moment, a townsman or woman would ask him what he was waiting for. At first Gova explained that they must be very careful not to repeat the mistakes of the city, and should benefit from the trials and errors of other settlements. This pleased the people to hear, and they afforded him more time to work. Time passed, but there were still no signs of sparks. They began again, at opportune moments, to catch Gova and politely inquire about the future. The answers, as the years rolled on, became shorter and vaguer, but still managed to charge their aspirations with refreshed hope.

He left to travel, and apprenticed as an electrician. After a few years he returned with a great impatience. Soon after his return he got into an argument with the village fisherman, probably about measurements and accomplishments, and Gova shot him dead. The argument was never understood because Gova never discussed it. As the village now gathered in its center-most field, still he refused to discuss it.

The older men could still remember the previous hearing. It had taken place two generations ago, and involved the rape of a cripple who sat watching the sun set by the river everyday. An older man stood up and reminded the crowd that that culprit had been sent over the mountain and into the city for a hard hearing. And was hanged there. The two generations below the old man felt that the city had become dreadful at making decisions, and that they should deal with the problem, that day and in that field.

In the back row, a woman in linen shoes quietly tore up a length of sod from the ground. It was getting late, and damp, and cold. She tucked her feet into the ground, lay back on her elbows and gazed into the stars, wondering why nothing ever happened. Three inches below her little linen shoe, the last heart muscle of the very last Wallaby mole expired. The soil around it was black, dense, and cold, and thus absorbed its final, infinitesimal 'thwop!' like a mussel who filters a molecule of sea filth from its mass without a thought.

III – The entropy of lemonade

"Step *away* from the red line!" ordered an unlovable voice from a police megaphone.

Mr Ulrich abandoned his efforts to push through the people to see it, and retired on a block of concrete. He sat with the crowd in his eyes, and watched the faces of the people closely. They were verging on a riot. He smoothed his thin hair over to one side, which had a cooling effect that mimicked his late wife's touch, and had become a comfortable habit since her death. He often sat with his hands clasped, one gently rubbing the other to sustain a lost affection. It was as though he were divided right down the middle, one side taking over from where his wife left off. He carefully stretched his knees out, afraid that one of these days, they might pop off. It had been a long morning, and he had made the three blocks from his apartment to the protest in the hot Spring sun. His suit was beginning to soak through at the back, behind his shoulders.

People had been protesting the red line for centuries, which Mr Ulrich found foolish. He went for a lemonade at the coffee shop across the street to tell them so. As he stepped into the street, a car blew a red light to avoid the rocks being thrown at it. Ulrich had to admit he loved the anarchy. A thirsty protester was resting his elbows on the bar.

"Getting anywhere this year?" Ulrich was happy to engage a dissident.

The protester was spent. "They actually brought the fucking army in this time."

Ulrich could see that one of the protester's eyes was a bit bloody. His heart broke, at the mercy of all the sorts of stupidity it encountered.

"Look, it's a good party, an admirable thing, all of you. But that line's longer than forever and deeper than hell. It's always been there. It doesn't go just because you tell it to... what nonsense, all of you – it's a force of nature!" Mr Ulrich put his lips around his straw and, like a mud-caked, road-weary elephant, sucked his whole glass of lemonade in one continuous slurp.

Outside, the riot had exploded. Thousands were digging at the red line, and setting gas fires in its trenches. The army were defending themselves and collecting fire starters in their trucks. A few miles away, in a government institution, people were being punished.

IV – The cows

As far as anyone could see, the red line was continuous, endless. If a mission ever had been organized to follow it, the belief in its infinity would have been abandoned, for on a Nordic island, in a humid valley, a beautiful old cow lies in the grasses and rolls the end of the line around in her supple mouth. The point at which her tongue becomes the red line and the red line becomes her tongue is indistinguishable.

In Norse mythology, there is a cow by the name of Audhumla, who is said to have nourished the god Aurgelmir with her milk. She herself fed on salty stones, which she gradually licked into the first shape of man.

In recent years, a new protein disease has spread throughout Europe. The minuscule villain is a pathogen whose nature is unknown. It beckons its way into the fibres of cow meat, and turns the brains of those who eat it into Swiss cheese. It is almost indestructible, and survives many processes to contaminate the by-products of cows, which include carpeting, television sets and plastics. It can sleep in soil for 50 years; waiting to rise to the defense of the cows.

Post script – the other end

At the end of the Washington Mall, a totem of military defense stands erect; a symbolic projectile aimed at the sky; at the world. Two red lights ominously blink from its top, presumably the vision of the beast, or if not, then silent detonation meters, recording all the collisions of the cosmos. A boy of about 12 stands before it and decides that yes, that's what it must be doing.

A strikingly similar totem ushers the museumgoers, a few hundred metres away, into the entrance of the Smithsonian Museum of Natural History. It is a small-scale replica of the monument, disguised with paint, bars, numbers and animal silhouettes depicting a facile timeline of evolution. Settled at the base are variations of the single cell aquatic creatures. The halfway mark sports colorful illustrations of whales, and then horses. Near the top is a red line, just below the pyramid that crowns it. The pyramid is representation of the last ten million years of animal life, and depicts the newest species – the crowning jewel of natural selection: Man.

The pyramid is a shape of which only mankind is expert. It is built upon itself until it disappears, and leaves nothing below but a tomb. The wealth of the single cell spawned a billion years of evolution, of creatures that were born of and died back into the earth.

The red line is a tempting threshold, whispering a desperate plea to be crossed.

Beyond the red line is discomfort – that which separates our coming from our going. That which has sucked from the totem like a straw and has swallowed. That which is so consuming that it does not die back into the earth, but has its remains basted in formaldehyde and lain aside like a rubber tire, waiting to be devoured by the simple heat of the sun.

Pelicans at the weir, Saskatoon

by Jen Hadfield

(for Ian Banks)

Don't you want to hum Tuxedo Junction
when they chug up to the weir?
– their vanilla slacks, their teetotal eggnog,
the bland grace of 1920s gangsters?
Night coming on, Venus up, and they hang on the roulette eddy,
tamping down fluff with beaks so long
it's like opening mail with an epée,
they skoosh water up to their armpits,
they cruise the narrow beam from your floodlight
that cuts a strip from the river as green, as straight
as nori. And then they dive, in unison.

Oh, Luck
– be a Lady!

Modern Maid

Christine Hamm

Joan of Arc works at the Gap.
Her armor, nearly invisible under
the florescent light, catches on the sweaters
she folds, so that cashmere threads
follow her everywhere, a crimson cape.

She can't remember how she got here:
most days, can't remember her name when she gets up,
but knows where her keys are,
and what bus to take to work.

God speaks to her sideways,
flickering reflections in the
napkin dispenser at the diner,
upside down when she licks
the ice cream clean from her spoon.

Joan sees pinions behind her when she uses the ATM.
There's angels, sometimes angry and frightening,
often white, and always in her dreams.
They smell like straw and milk...

Joan is sixteen. She's always sixteen.
She's so blond her eyebrows disappear.
She has freckles and is serious,
chews off her lipstick.
She'll heal you if you ask nice,
and go back behind the 501s with her.
Her name means "God is gracious."
Sometimes when she's stacking the perfume
called heaven
she remembers this is true.

The river is far behind us

Paul Hardacre

like ovens, she wooden ranks the years
& light (jarred or elemental/boys with
bloody heads & drained, veiled

     the red hose his life & dirt

          vacant, suspicious
          behaviour
          (hands &

sky up near basra, umm qasr

some kind

      of powder
mixed & heated eyes
          of her sons burning dolls
          out back) MYSTERY points

over the trench

the world psoriatic & clawed her missing
brother –

   *

& true stories, conjoined robert redfords ('the naturals')
are found dead (one is a puppeteer with his

     mouth taped; the other a taxi
     driver who has
     been stabbed)

     & hawkeye is tested for allergies /
        barbaric telegraph
            magical landing aged

seven

staring, the orange ball fast asleep
& walks through the door / the steel-capped gift
      he bears it
      clutched for

           fear of skins in
           spring hill falklands sick iron lady

   *

fingers on buttons &
phones rubber generals on
sticks (model jump-jets in
      gunmetal, commandos /
         crafted dust &
         TV empty box
another downed life the eastern plains as toohey
                         forest burns

                we dump
                   stolen bikes & front-kick
         black boys / part of a bong
         secreted in guttering
         buried flagons filled with
            piss (actual?

   *

occupation:
         belfast method, giggling & shackled
         resistance mural or shit

on a wall / black guard of...

         childhood intubated & ringing
         a bell the year of *lone wolf* &
         beautiful afternoons thought he
            was dead or too real

fingers grease & cap / everything fits –
> this house this daily guess
> at money each image takes
> hours, the same jokes & we drive
> his stumps & bulbs the speed
> of prince the mags at least are cool

*

mention patchuko or corazon
> the joinedwords make it
>> smoke & ditch

>> peeled affect & gleeson's frontal tube
>> life cockled & flew
>>> in her mire all winter
> he lounged or shook/noted clouds &
>> birds (spangled drongo,
>>> butcher bird

>> pied & grey, his painted tent & hide
>> an hour from moran's falls
>> small snakes, tomahawk
>> reading *fighting fantasy 14* ('temple of terror')

> it rains & draws/everything struggles

he throttles a bird by accident

No better a house

Kenneth J Harvey

For Josiah Boyde Harvey

A man from the government stood in the doorway of Ace Winslow's one-room shack. He had arrived on a silver snowmobile and wore a silver helmet and silver zip-up snowsuit that was peculiar to the area. After introducing himself, he stood silent for a few moments, awaiting conversation that was not forthcoming, then said: "We'll be building you a new house in the spring." He explained that Ace need not live in "this place" any longer, that the government had initiated programs to ensure that the people in Cutland Junction lived better lives. Ace had never seen the man before. He nodded regardless and grinned and asked the man in for a mug of tea, but the man said he was busy and had better get going. Many more stops to make before the day was out.

"On government land over there," the man had indicated, pointing his silver mitt toward the white featureless expanse of barrens so that Ace had no idea how far. The snow went on for a vast stretch of distance, leading to the far away shadow of Coombs Hill and its deep woods where Ace had worked the trap line for over fifty years. "Here's some papers explaining the program." The man stuck his mitt under his arm and yanked out his hand. Ace was surprised at how pink and smooth the hand was. He watched it as the man pulled out a thick booklet from his deep zip-up pocket. "If you have any questions," said the man, passing the booklet to Ace, "I'll be back in a few weeks." The man then looked over his shoulder and all around as though wondering what the house might be doing plunked down there in the middle of nothing but white.

Ace grinned some more and nodded. He weighed the booklet in his hand, marvelling at how thick and full of words it was. He then watched the man turn to watch the snow that had begun falling an hour ago. "It's getting worse," said the man from the government. He fitted on his helmet and fastened the strap beneath his chin.

Ace winked in sturdy agreement and clutched the booklet with his brown leathery fingers. The cover was shiny and featured a drawing of a brand new house with a big leafy green tree to either side of it. The government man turned and climbed on his snowmobile, tugged the ignition cord and gave a wave before heading off across the white barrens toward the frozen surface of Black Duck Lake.

Ace could see a few dry bush twigs where they were poked up through the snow and cracked off in the path of the snowmobile. He shut his door and went over to the pot-bellied stove. Lifting the damper off the front burner, he admired the pure redness of the fire roaring within, then stuffed the booklet into the perfect circle.

He nodded and grinned, the lines at the corners of his eyes deepening as he poked at the paper with the fire iron. "A fine heat," he assured himself, feeling the hot surge so full against his face that he leaned slightly away and slid the heavy damper back over to seal the hole.

In the spring, the workers came. Ace watched them survey the land about sixty feet across the barrens where they were driving stakes and measuring the spaces between one man and the other. What they were doing required great precision. A small shift to the left and back. A tiny shift to the right and forward.

The men wore spring clothes and this pleased Ace to see that another season was coming. If he were a younger man, he'd be off in the woods, cutting and hauling wood to sell around Cutland Junction, down Shearstown Line and in Bareneed. From his doorway, he watched the workers stretch long runs of tape from one point to another, then mark the driven stakes with bits of red ribbon that flapped lightly in the breeze. Fine work, Ace told himself. Work like that was hard to come by. He considered those stakes, imagining himself yanking their sharp points out of the ground and carrying them back to his shack. They were just the right size for burning.

A few days later, a bulldozer arrived in the early hours, the roar of its engine startling Ace when he was lifting the blackened tin kettle to make his tea. The dozer had been delivered on a flatbed truck that was parked on the makeshift dirt road the men had laid to get to him. In no time, the bulldozer cleared the land, the clay fresh and brownish-red in mounds and then levelled. No trees to worry about. Too bad. Ace could have sawed them up and burned them. Even now, heading toward summer, the nights were nippy. Ace had to keep a fire burning, his bones remembering the trap line, having to keep the small stove going in the numbing outdoors night, or die. The main thing was to make it through the night without freezing to death. Just keep warm and remember where the food was buried, pray that an animal hadn't dug it up and eaten it so that a part of your life was eaten away with it.

The earth beneath the snow. Ace always wondered on that when he was snowshoeing through the trapline, the fur of the caribou skins soft against his skin. The crunch and vivid brilliance of the snow as his breath steamed out of him. The warm earth beneath that snow. It gave him consolation and blessed his sleep.

In the late afternoon of that same day, the bulldozer was loaded back on the truck bed and taken away. Ace watched out his window as everyone left in their vehicles. The freshly disturbed earth was a strange sight, a deep-brown specific space surrounded by the soggy immenseness of brittle blonde, burgundy and green barrens.

It was another two days before a different crew of workers showed up to start sawing and hammering. Supplies were delivered by big trucks that often got stuck and needed to be hauled out by other vehicles that eventually got stuck too until a crane was brought on site and kept there to help the vehicles free themselves from the clamp of the earth.

A great deal of sawing and hammering started in, and, eventually, the stud frames of walls were put together on the floor of the house and then raised and nailed down. The roofless wooden frame was erected sixty feet away from Ace's shack. The perfect ribs of the house.

Ace would rise from where he was having a lie-down on his daybed and stand next to his table, his old knees aching, until he had to sit in a chair and peek out the bottom rim of the window. All the while, he would watch the blonde-wood frame, admiring the exact fit of the construction. Occasionally, one of the workmen would come over on his break and stand in Ace's doorway and chat while he wiped sweat from his forehead. The men all knew of Ace, how he had lived alone for years, how men from the community would drop off fish and caribou steaks, potatoes and carrots, because Ace was respected for surviving and twining together the legends that figured his life. The workers were thankful to have the steady work that the government was providing by hiring them to build these new houses in and around the community.

"Same old t'ing," said Ace. "Build'n houses fer us."

The workers would smile or laugh openly. "Can't complain about the work though," they'd say, respectfully.

"No," Ace would agree with an understanding intake of breath. "Can't complain 'bout dat, me son."

The men went about their business. Ace knew many of them from the area, others were from places far from the woods, off along the coast. Over time, he learned that he was even related to a few of the local ones. He knew the stories of their lives or he invented what he could not recall and told it all back to them in yarns. The sawing and hammering made him remember.

It was nice of the men to be helping out. He watched from the window while he sipped his tea. One day to the next. The workers toiled with speed and efficiency. Hammering and sawing, and calling out requirements. The way they worked made Ace feel proud. They were good men to work so hard. They knew what they were doing, willing to learn more every day because they were interested in figuring themselves stronger; old-timers in the making.

At night, Ace would leave his doorway and, guided by his dim flashlight, wander across the pitch-black barrens to the site of his new house. The smell of fresh wood and upturned clay hung in the air like a natural intrusion. He would sweep the flashlight beam over the erected two-by-four studs and see the light travel between them, faintly spread against the night sky. He strolled back and forth in the darkness, collecting the scraps of two-by-four and two-by-six left over from the day's work. He collected them in his arms and walked with the flashlight beam aimed at the ground a few feet ahead of his slow stride.

Coming into his shack from the outside, he felt as though he were entering a foreign place. The warm light from the oil lamp softened the shape of the objects in the room in a way that made him feel attached in his heart to them. He'd lay the bits of wood on his kitchen table and leave to collect more. Next to his stove, there was a deep closet outfitted with shelves. On these shelves, Ace neatly stacked the ends of wood, brushing the bits of sawdust away with a neat sweep of his fingertips.

The house was completed in four weeks, the roof shingles gummed and nailed as the crowning touch. Sitting there on the barrens, the house appeared solid and whole, but hopelessly, senselessly vacant.

A silver pickup truck with a government sign on the door arrived and parked on the new dirt road. The government man got out and stood a moment staring at the house, his hands on his hips, then he knocked on Ace's door and announced – with a proud smile – that Ace could move in any time he liked. He handed the old man a silver ring with two shiny gold-coloured keys on it. "This one is for the lock on the front door, and this one's for the lock on the back."

Ace took the ring of keys, nodded and invited the man in for a mug of tea, but the man was in a hurry. "Another time," the government man assured Ace, but didn't mean it, so that Ace shut the door without further thought. He studied the keys as he went and stood by the window. The government man climbed back into his truck and drove away. The keys were brand-new-shiny where he laid them on the table top. Ace wondered why they had locked the house. Why it had two doors. Easy to walk in the front, tread straight through the house, and then out the back. Nothing there to stop a man from simply passing through.

Two weeks later, the government man arrived for another visit. He was driving the same silver pickup truck with the government markings on its door. Most of the truck was clean but the bottom was caked with mud and dust.

"Did you need help moving?" the government man asked, pointing toward the new pale-green bungalow with brown shutters that sat unoccupied on the barrens. The workers had planted two small trees in the front yard, one at either side of the house. They had even built a wooden fence and painted it white.

Ace shook his head, "Oh, no, me son. Not at all."

"I can get a few people to lend a hand."

"Don't be so foolish. No need of dat."

"Will you be moving soon?"

Ace winked and grinned, "Don't know. I were jus' look'n."

"Oh? Looking? At what?"

"Dat house, da new one. Ye couldn't 'av missed it."

The government man glanced over Ace's shoulder. "Is your wife at home?" he asked.

"Wife?"

"You're not married?"

"Yer a queer fellow, ye know," said Ace, "Right hard ta talk ta."

The government man said nothing, and Ace shut the door.

The next day, a different man in a silver truck arrived to tell Ace that he had to be moved by the end of the week. "Otherwise," the man said in a husky voice, "We'll be forced to condemn your house."

"Over dere?" Ace asked, light-heartedly.

"No," said the man. "This one." The man was outfitted in caribou skins and seal-skin boots despite the warming weather. He was a big man with a big face and green eyes. He stared past Ace's shoulder into the kitchen with the daybed where Ace slept, then his eyes took in Ace's face. He spent a few moments appreciating the features. "If you move on your own, we won't need to tear this place down. Although we might need to anyway. I'm not certain."

Ace shook his head. "Ye remember dis house?" he asked, tilting his head toward the roof.

"How you mean?"

"Dis house were built fer me, too."

"When?"

"I don't 'av a clue. How da bejeezuz am I supposed ta know? Where ye frum any-way? Yer frum down on da coast."

"I'm from St Shotts."

"Christ hallmighty. Why'd ye come dis far?"

"It's my job."

Ace scoffed and began shutting his door, but the man continued, "Just like fish-ermen used to sail up to the Labrador for the salmon, or head out to the ice fields for seals. What's the difference? I just work for the government. Work is work. I have to come here."

This line of reasoning gave Ace pause and he invited the man in for a mug of tea. The man accepted and they engaged in a lengthy conversation about travel by boat which greatly pleased Ace. Then the man glanced at his watch and glanced out the window and said, "I best be going. Other stops to make."

Ace nodded and showed the man to the door. It was a beautiful afternoon. The two men stood in the doorway, facing the sky, silenced by and drawn into its immense blueness.

"Nice talking," the man finally said and offered Ace his hand. Ace looked at it and it was dark and scarred. He took hold of it and gave it a firm shake.

"Pleasure," he said, shaking the man's hand a few more times for good measure. "Yer a fine feller, ye are. Drop by fer a visit any time ye likes."

The next day, Ace woke to hear the wind howling. He shuffled from his daybed and opened the door, gripping it tightly against the strain of the wind. He went to his outhouse to relieve himself, then, with the wind pressing against him, he pushed on across the barrens to the new house. The back door was locked. He fished around in the pocket of his green work pants and found the ring of two keys. The first one he tried fit perfectly. He opened the door and stepped in out of the wind to face the utter calmness of the back porch. The smell of new paint and fresh emptiness gave him pause. He felt as though he did not belong and might be caught intruding.

Listening, he heard nothing, not even the howl of the wind beyond the walls. His boot steps echoed through the entire house as he stepped into the kitchen. There was a new electric stove and refrigerator and plenty of cupboards. There was a chrome kitchen set. Ace sat in one of the vinyl-covered chairs and found it small on his rump, uncomfortable and slippery. He went back to his house and began dismantling his pot-bellied stove. He carried it piece by piece to the new house, recalling how he had to lug his smaller stove around with him on the trapline, always lugging and needing the stove to eat a meal and drive the chill away.

The electric stove was attached by a thick orange wire that had to be yanked again and again to get loose. It finally snapped free from somewhere under the floorboards. Ace shoved the electric stove out into the back yard where it tipped and rattled violently onto its back. Retrieving his wooden tool box from his shack, he cut a precise hole in the wall of the new house where the stove pipe could be snugly fitted.

The house was warm. He had water that ran from the taps. A pump that brought it from a well that was capped at the side of the house. It was fine living there although somewhat fake like it wasn't really his life at all that he was wandering around in.

As it grew colder, the pump stopped working and the two toilets wouldn't flush. Ace went to his outhouse, which had been left standing as an historical marker by the demolition crew. The squat compartment smelled the same as always. There was no changing that. It smelled like a permanent part of his life that no one could ever tear down.

"Sacred ground," he muttered, sitting there, grunting.

In the late fall, Ace ran out of the scrap lumber he had collected and began wishing the demolition crew hadn't carted away all the wood from his old house. As soon as the fire began ebbing and the chill became obvious, he opened the door that led out into the living room and surveyed the furnishings. He began sawing up the two big chairs. He worked up a sweat which was fine because the living room was cold and he didn't like lingering in the sharpness of the air without moving. The cold of the living room put him in mind of the vicious outside. He carried the wood from the upholstered chairs into the kitchen and shut the door, began splitting the wood with his handaxe.

Fire raging, he decided to make a narrower bed of the boxspring that rested on the floor in his new bedroom. The bedroom, down a short hallway and next to the bathroom, was always cold, too far from the kitchen to ever properly heat.

In November, Ace began ripping out the bedroom walls, first burning the moldings and then the closet door. When nothing but ashes remained, he tore up the cumbersome carpet and commenced hauling up the bedroom floorboards that were nice and thick.

Ace sat in the kitchen, in the chair he had salvaged from his old shack before the workers tore it apart, plank by plank. He looked at the empty chrome chairs and wondered why they were there. His old wooden table was sitting in the living room, looking out of place among all the new woodless things.

In the dim stove-light of the kitchen, Ace thought of getting up to feed the languishing fire. Glancing around the walls, he studied the cupboards. Why had they put doors on the cupboards? You couldn't see inside that way.

Ace pushed himself to his feet and pulled open the last remaining drawer where a few of his tools were stored. He found his screwdriver right beside his hammer where he had left it. The hinges were something he might someday use. He unscrewed them, then took down his handaxe from where it was hung on the knife rack the workers had put there for him. He set the cupboard doors on the table, stood them up, one at a time, and easily split them down into manageable pieces. Good and dry. The wood burned evenly, crackled the way he liked to remember the twigs burning on the trapline.

The four chrome chairs were no good for burning. The table was equally useless. He tossed them out the back door and replaced the table with the one from his shack. Ace watched out the back window, studied the two men who had come to haul away the electric stove. They set it on the back of their pickup truck and tied it down with green rope, then wandered around, surveying what was left of the house. Ace waved at them when they returned and looked his way before climbing into their truck. The two men waved back while the engine started with a rumble.

Ace cast his scrupulous gaze around the kitchen. Nothing left to burn. He commenced tearing the clapboard off the front of the house. It burned furiously as it was dried by the sun and coated in paint. Next, he commenced tearing out the front porch. The front door burned nicely. Thick solid wood, hard to saw. The casing around the door came away easily, and then the closet door, the porch's box of walls, and then the front wall disappearing to give him an open view of the yard and the fence. In the livingroom, he took the large window out, lowered it with rope and left it on the ground for anyone who needed it, then beat out the full front wall. Nice to be sheltered with a roof over his head like that but for it to be wide open before him too; the outdoors just there at the lip of the living room. The flooring under the carpet would give him enough wood to last a month or more.

Back in the kitchen, Ace tore up the linoleum to admire what was underneath.

The echoing sound his boots made against the wood was more fitting than the hushed sound they made treading over linoleum.

One morning, snow fell and buried all the trash in the back yard. The snow melted the next day, revealing everything as it was. But then, the following day, it snowed again and stayed that way for the rest of winter. Everything covered. Ace went for a walk in the small front yard. He stayed within the fence and looked out around, an immense field of white in all directions. He began hammering loose the planks from the fence. Occasionally, after one of the fence planks fell, he'd stop to turn and admire the way the snow clung to the limbs of the two small evergreens. How long for them to grow tall? he'd keep asking himself. "Christ, I'll be good'n dead by den."

Once the gyprock ceilings were pounded out of the living room, hallway, bathroom and bedrooms, the criss-cross of truss beams was revealed in explicit detail. Ace dragged his wooden table from the kitchen into the living room and stood on it, his head up in the squat attic. The trick was to figure out which supports could be cut away without the roof crashing down on him. He was still considering this as the winter began to loosen its grip. The roof was a hazard he would rather avoid. He decided to set his sights down instead of up, and so lowered himself into the spaces between the floor joists and began sawing them away. Two-by-sixes. Avoid the galvanized nails. They would dull his saw, and where would he be with a dull saw?

In the spring, as the debris was uncovered, people from the community came to salvage what they could. They had been expecting this. A new house for Ace Winslow. A few of them tapped on Ace's back door to ask for his permission.

"Yays, take whatever ye desires," he'd reply, then stand in the doorway, overseeing the men and women going about their business. "Nothing ta me," he'd mutter, watching the junk be hauled away by the thankful lot who came in need of it.

A few months later, in the early summer, the government man who had engaged Ace in a welcome bit of intelligent conversation the previous fall dropped by for a visit. He brought a house-warming gift, a shiny-leafed plant of the sort Ace had never seen before.

"It's a rubber plant," the government man told Ace, baffled by the sight of what was left of the new house, the roof trusses perilously extended over blank space toward the front, the walls of the other rooms cut down. The outer wall of the kitchen, once the living room wall, had wallpaper still stuck to it that flapped in the wind, facing the elements.

"Looks fake," Ace told the man, watching the plant where the man set it on the table and commenced staring around the kitchen.

"I brought it from St Shotts," he said, distracted. "What happened here?"

"Needed ta keep warm."

The man laughed outright. "There's electric heat here," he explained, pointing to the thermostat on the wall.

"Wha's dat?"

"It's electric heat," the man told Ace, taking a seat.

"Bullcrap," said Ace. "Ye care fer a mug of tea?" He slid the kettle onto the damper. "We can 'av a gab."

"Why not, it's nice and warm in here." The man joined his hands on the table and smiled. "Comfortable." He rubbed his rough fingers over one of the plant's shiny leaves.

"Canned milk good enough fer ye?"

The man nodded, then laughed through his nostrils and shook his head.

"Wha's so funny?"

"Nothing, nothing. I'm just laughing at me."

"Ye gonna build me anudder house?"

"You bet," said the government man, giving Ace a generous wink. "Only this time we'll know better. We'll make it even bigger."

Ace dug a deep hole in the back yard. It took him two weeks to finish it, his knees gave him trouble as the hole got further down and he had to climb into it and then paw his way up and out. He'd puff and curse as he'd exert himself, then stand and catch his breath. Leaning on his shovel or pick handle, he'd stare down into the hole.

Ace dismantled his outhouse, moved it – piece by piece – over the new hole and nailed it back together. He scraped the remaining bits of wallpaper off the outer walls of the kitchen and painted the one-room house with one of the tins of paint the workers left in the back porch. They had left a few brushes, too, in a bucket of water that had frozen but was now thawed.

When the painting was finished, Ace stepped back to have a look. This house was no better a house than his old one. In fact, it was worse. The kitchen was bigger, harder to heat. No benefit to him at all. He did, however, pride himself in the pair of little spruce trees. They never failed to give him a rush of both promise and pleasure. Watching those two evergreens, he took great delight in imagining himself a much smaller man.

Address book

Steven Heighton

Bad luck, it's said, to enter your own name
and numbers in the new address book.
All the same, as you slowly comb
through the old one for things to pick

out and transfer, you are tempted to coin
yourself a sparkling new address,
new name, befitting the freshness of this clean-
slating, this brisk kiss

so long to the heart-renders – every friend
you buried or let drift, those Home for the Aged
maiden relations, who never raged
against the dying of anything, and in the end

just died. An end to the casualties pressed
randomly between pages – smudged, scribbled chits
with lost names, business cards with their faded
bold fronts of confidence, solvency. The palimpsest

time made of each page; the hypocrite it made
of you. Annie, whom you tried two years to love
because she was straight-hearted, lively, and in love
with you (but no strong-arming your cells and blood);

Mad Carl, who typed poet-to-poet squibs in the pseudo-
hickish, hectoring style of Pound, all sermonfire
and block caps, as AINT FIBRE ENOUGH HERE, BOYO,
BACK TO THE OLE FLAX FIELD... this *re* a score

of your nature poems. When he finally vanished
into the far east, you didn't mind the silence.
Still, this guilt, as if it weighs in the balance,
every choice – as if each time your pen banished

a name it must be sensed somewhere, a ballpoint stab, hex-

needle to the heart, the treacherous
innocent *no* of Peter, every X
on the page a turncoat kiss...

Bad luck, it's said, to enter your own name in the new
book – as if, years on, in the next culling,
an executor will be leafing through and calling
or sending word to every name but you.

November

Kevin Higgins

November rampages down the avenue,
like a gang of victorious soldiers,
drunk but still thirsting for more,
eager now the slaughter comes easy.

And Winter's bare face glares
everywhere at us. The balding trees,
all along the street, suddenly synchronise
their watches, and admit defeat.

Poetics

Paul Hoover

I have no objectives, no system, no tendency, and no plan.
I have no speech, no tongue, no memory, and no realm.
Because nothing matters, I am consistent, committed, and excited.
I prefer the definite, the bounded, the repressed and the weak.
Not objectivity but neutrality of being.
Not spontaneity but panic.
For only seeing believes and only the body thinks.
For success is common to those who fail.
For the world's beauty is fading because the world is fading.
For the best narrative is always oblique.
For thought only thinks it thinks – all has been foretold.
For without cruelty, there would be no beauty.
For kindness is always a little bit tragic.
For the mind's progress is zig-zag and stabs at every tree.
For the best art makes things disappear.

After Gerhard Richter, 2002

The Orientalist

Ranjit Hoskote

He went back to drafting policies of state
but never forgot the courtesan in the Sanskrit play.

She wrote him letters on pages folded
in triangles like betel leaves

but did not wait for the beloved and spring;
creepers soothed her, her lamp-lit hours passed

among the scented shadows of lovers.

At the roadblock

Halvard Johnson

Vastly abandoned, the eskers and terminal
moraines of southern Finland made for diverse
and enjoyable reading. Edmund, by comparison, is
a bore, and, sadly, only one of many there.

Almost seamlessly, snow cleared by ploughing,
they wind across the glaciated countryside, tunneling,
sometimes, under the ice, becoming more or less
filled with wash when the ice melts.

Positively slashing, among the occasionally puzzled
relics of doorsteps and yardworks, setting aside
completely, push having come to shove, their pre-
conceptions of the shifting nature surrounding them.

Ultimately redoubtable, the double-minded farmer
gives rise to fear, even to dread, and is thus to be
respected, at least for the moment, beyond his
(or her) ability to do us severe and actual damage.

Up there

Fred Johnston

After Le Zénith, *by Sully Prudhomme, 1875*

Like the mad Austrian whose wings flail and fail,
Absurd, a joke, even in the way he drops
From a second's hesitation – the camera takes
A pinch of dust of his death between the girly legs
Of the Eiffel Tower – it must have been something,
A balloon like a brandy glass made of air,
What was visible from up there was the world laid bare.

A soft lung closes on itself; too high and far,
Too bright, as if facing down God on a mountain
Of cloud – everything's invisible now,
And there's nothing left to breathe –
The fire's dowsed, the little brazier blackens,
His hands are full of sand: eight thousand metres
Is as high as the soul flies: the basket swings to the beat
Of those two others, dead weights, at his feet.

Garden

Jill Jones

Never said is the wound.
Expectation always remains, taking the night.
A false rain drapes the garden.
Does one love remain in the many?

There was excellence, & rumour & endings.
It is beyond this garden now.
A story dances across the floor.
Expectation takes on the night.

Each time is a different visit of the same.
Floorboards are beyond repetition.
Dust curls into silence.
Night twitches in expectation, taken too far.

Because of what was said, it wasn't said.
A devoted rain washes the silence.
The many in one is the kiss.
Expectation always remains.

Serir

Norman Jope

From Suspended gold – Saharan pistes

And then there is *serir*. A cleansed space, a location wind whistles through, arranging the remains. A somewhere else, where nothing prevails and the horizons are constant.

We can only define it by moving slowly. There are no nests for the arrows that fall.

This is a space where silence enters the pilgrim – enshrines the one who renounces action and event. A surface of refusal reaches into the refusal that is death, a domain where every gobbet of flesh is razored directly from bone.

Its tenuous gravel is arranged on pallid sand, beneath a sky in which nothing, not even the human eye, is tangible. Its expanses erode all primate curiosity, returning the mind to reptilian languor. The brain is spring-cleaned, as if by an injection of menthol.

Each stone here is a ka'aba, the tiny temple of a posthumous grace, on which a black sweat drips from marmoreal bones. They turn to gold, then scarlet, in the light that dismantles them.

Coming here means to assent to a deeper nakedness, in which all flesh is superfluous. A heap of bones at the bottom of the star-well, one is filleted by photonic vultures.

Knowledge, here, is scorched. Belief, ignited.

We are suddenly here, where the music stops, and the invention of the Names of God begins.

Wasp

Jayne Fenton Keane

A wasp dangles

airborne origami –
holes in its wings

attracted to glass
angry at the bright orange

dangling, shiny
earring – full of threats.

A man mows grass.
A woman mows grass.

Wasp is disoriented
by noise. A recipe

for *something's*
going to happen.

The child peddles to and fro.
A flash of chrome on her wrist

medic-alert bracelet
catching the sun.

Child doesn't see wasp.
Wasp is attracted to

colourful bicycle tassels
streaming. Chrome spokes

flash, the child's hair flows.
The word WASP itches in a rash

underneath the medic-alert bracelet.

The child can't breathe
laughing and peddling
so hard. The wasp

untidy, dangles. A sprinkler
turns on. The girl

smells birthday candles
on the breeze.

a mother instead

W B Keckler

what if strength is forgetting.
and only that.
how disappointing then a god who was fire.
who was fire-speaking.
his disappointment over the world.
what if the world is all by itself
growing more beautiful animals.
such arabesques. fire-feathered wings
claws. fins. crests. craniums. eyes
that can trace the journey back
thousands of miles over black ocean.
growing stronger. through eons.
by letting go of everything
but what is before them.
flaming moment. that does not speak
unless they move, unless they launch
their bodies into it. hear their own cries
as they swim through time. are buoyed by time and are it.
yes. oblivion beneath them like a mother.
birth and death both. her body a universe-membrane.
unable to distinguish new babe from old body skeletonizing.
feeling both as time. feeding and forgetting. her comfort in comfort.

Sex in the confines

Amy King

I was in the next door bar sober
by you standing one night suddenly
a desperado among the people,
a tall boy upon your strict girl
approach, never the one to go
to hands that hardly burn or
give into submission. Shall
we count on even digits in
the bathroom line? We do and
a cloak of incense suits Hart Crane's
sleep. Within his sea drowning
briefcase still exists handwritten
pillow manuals: how to fertilize
and rain haloes from the color
of light. Keep writing skins
of homemade poems pressed
to the rims of open salt cans. I pass
off your vodka tonic for this palm
wrung dark thin blue, discuss
welcome mat grass green, always
skipping the reach of private tentacles
to lean out & gather over your space.

Boxing gloves

Chris Kinsey

Handed to me for amnesty –

these veterans pucker on the shelf
like a couple who've taken their teeth
out to be comfortable.

Blood-burst red,
the outer skin's soft
as skin stretched over fontanelles.

The linings' shredded strings
are a clench on the throat tendons
of the boy conscript you silenced.

Punch-drunk on sweat
poundings and jabs didn't
knock the replays cold.

Putting them on's a fumble into
puppet-darkness

a scrabble back
into the foxhole of a Falklands spring –

the shock of ripping awake from a garotte

your best mate shrieking bayonet steel.

Sorry

Roddy Lumsden

When I hurt you and cast you off, that was buccaneer work:
the sky must have turned on the Bay that day and spat.
We'd tarried on corners, we'd dallied on sofas, we were
in progress, do you see? Yet stormcloud bruises bloomed

where once we touched. The walls swam under minty fever;
we failed to reach the long, low sleep of conquerors.
Since I played wrong and you did too, since we were wrong,
we need apologies; for your part in this sorry slip of hearts,

you should walk on Golden Hill at night alone; for mine
I will hang with my enemies, out on the long shore,
our brigand bodies impaled on the thorns of our failures,
the cold day casting draughts through our brinkled bones.

A tale of two Sickerts

Alexis Lykiard

"I have always been a literary painter, thank goodness, like all the decent painters" – Sickert to
Virginia Woolf
*"American crime writer Patricia Cornwell is convinced she has solved the mystery of Jack the
Ripper's identity... She bought up 31 of Sickert's works... Cornwell actually tore up one Sickert
canvas in her search for clues... According to Cornwell, the paintings contain clues to Sickert's
double life."* – Fortean Times, Feb 2002.

Every new century a connoisseur's relief
expands as he sets foot in France again
sauntering freely through this port
capricious Sickert so well knew
savouring its low-key sleazy nightlife.
Always the cafés, delicious quests
for *fruits de mer*, fishy stories, or a stew...
Whoever wanders past a capacious square
with its statue of the grand Duquesne,
will skirt the ugly Église St Jacques, where
ray be relished those drabber corners caught
reliably on canvas by the great

misfit, grim dauber of deadly *Ennui*.
Sickert the seedy and fastidious
dandy was bawdier than Baudelaire,
razor-sharp: highly influential he
appears, these macabre days of stress, to us.
(Micawberish and always strapped for cash
all artists can appreciate his fate!)
Drama, wit, disguises, W.S. liked –
sick humour suiting men of many tarts.
A chameleon addicted to music-halls.
Bold chancer, unexpected colourist.
Odd old buffer cutting a determined dash,

but keen to terminate unwelcome calls,
he was forced to work from photos, fast...
Most loath to settle his disputed bills,
Slippery recluse, he turned mysterious.
Hence, if not quite at home at 'St Peter's',
Sickert played Elderly Eccentric, psyched
out sad Denton Welch. (That poor youth still
produced his own cunning verbal portrait
afterwards – mordant, dark as anything
his vivid ancient model ever imagined.)
One recent essay posits a Royal fœtus,
imagines the handsome, wayward W.S.

as banished courtier doomed to years of exile
in Dieppe – no artist's proper life or style.
Debts are the surer bet; bastards; a French mistress –
these detained Sickert, who might well have faked
some joke in vile taste, like Jack the Ripper
secretly taking a last French leave...
Do clues, vestiges of guilt, litter the vague terrain
for truth-crazed researchers and the latterday tripper?
Dead giants exist, fit to entertain or receive
comic homage from gay scribes. Living in vain,
paint shrewdly rendered. Doubtful myths need proving:
vanished echoes, gaslit nights, the past unvarnished.

Enough of apple picking now

Don McGrath

Thank you, you shook my tree.
I lay supine
on the paid-for sofa.
I swam through water
that was more like steel.
"Don't be embarrassed," said the doctor,
"take the pills."

I took the pills. I found myself
standing at 3a.m.
before a burning house
by the General Hospital.
A surgical mask
was pressed into my hands.
"Put it on," said a voice,
"it's for the fumes."

I put it on
and watched, my legs
tangled in the hoses.
The flames
were clean against the sky.

Then I wandered home
through Upper Westmount
where my attire
elicited a threat.

Some thugs of privilege
had me figured
for a "faggot" – a faggot
coming from a fire.

Terzanelle for a killing

Nigel McLoughlin

There I was, standing on the height,
squinting toward the sun, my sight
blurred by the constant strain,

my tears rainbowed by the light.
I saw a hawk circle round his game,
catch the air, stand at eye-height

Not twenty yards distant. I swear
he plucked the bird clean and banked right,
strained his body to a blurred stain

in his dive as he swooped and righted,
turned and sped sunward like a ricochet
and left me standing on the height

astounded, short of breath, asway
(until I found my feet), breathing, delighted
that I had not stained my blurry brains

on the rocks below. With all my might
I flew down that hill like a man astray.
And the feeling, standing on that height,
blurred inside me like a muted strain.

Asylum seeker

Jo Mazelis

Cunningly disguised as human beings,
we step upon the displaced planet.
Our only difference
to your unsuspecting senses
might be a whiff
of unfamiliar jasmine oil
or the faintest suspicion of a broken
atom of cracked coriander seed
lodged beneath a finger nail.
That, and a darting shadow
scorched on the eye
of someone, somewhere
fled from,
and someone, somewhere
still loved.
And somewhere itself –
a place ever longed for
where birds and stones
and rivers know our names
and we, theirs.

From the intestines of a mystical dog

Valeria Melchioretto

My mother kept her Swiss watch in the remoteness
of the master bedroom, in her sacred wardrobe drawer;
in that handbag which looked like a legless black poodle
with two golden ears in the middle of its spine.

There it ticked more regularly than her heart
entangled with embroidered handkerchiefs,
crucifixes, Bibles, Holy Mary amulets and things
worth waiting for like; better days, sweet blessings
and the promised ever afters.

When my knees were free of plasters, which was rarely,
she granted me the privilege to be let into her shrine
almost close enough to touch that time which
she sheltered even from herself.

The poodle's magic died when one weekday
she gave that old mechanical watch to a better-behaved girl.

Sprinkler

Matthew Miller

"...stirring at night in little pleasure gardens" – Beckett, 'Molloy'

Slanting to answer, I can never quite splash you down.
In the guesswork, a surprise that sucks the fun away
burrows up through the quilt of pretty weeds. It pops
its grinning face through a hole cut in the playing board,
then another & another, as I revolve.

You have your own strenuous little game, based on
similar principles of chance & recurrence, and if you should say,
"forget it, just forget it," I'll ask you how (and we'll be stalemated)
watching as our arcs of conversation cross paths.
We should not be duped, despite the altitude of bluegrass
& dandelion: these are springs, pump, & plastic.

I thought we were going to grow, to rise higher
even than the tree-line, so that we could finally glimpse
the horizons of this country we've revolved in.
To see beyond the fields & roads, convening
on this cardstock castle. Now here come
the landscapers again. They're unrolling the turf.

Narration

Vivek Narayanan

All day he chased the producer
who was a busy man –
he cornered him at the studio
but barely shook his hand;

he stalked the lazy shoot outdoors
baked like a fruit in the sun,
but when there was a chance for words
the big man had to run;

at last at a certain concubine's
posh residence –
hanging by the gate, 11 p.m. –
he got an audience.

The luminary hawked loudly and
spat on the sidewalk;
then with a flick of his hand, he said,
"No script, o.k.? Just talk."

"The father's wife is brutally raped
and set on fire by
a politician, a banker and a gangster-rake;
the father takes his life" –

our man began at a rapid clip –
"The wife's twins, orphaned
and adopted by different families
(Hindu, Christian);

one grows up to be a policeman,
the other a roadside thug.
At first their lives are humdrum,
comical or snug –

they dance and sing in the gardens with their girlfriends,
get drenched in summer rain;
then they find each other and the fate of their mother
unlocking the door to pain.

"They team up to take revenge,
they learn the art of disguise;
practice their aim at the firing range
and perhaps polemicise."

"They take the villains one by one:
the banker is boiled alive,
the rake is hung by a hook in his foreskin
and, while taking a bribe

in the rather satisfying finale,
the politician is caught,
stripped naked and flayed before
he's simply shot."

This took five minutes to narrate
and, chewing thoughtfully,
the producer took ten more
before eventually

he said, "It's been done before and I'll
tell you straight – not
the gangster who lends me on call,
nor the banker that

launders my money clean nor
(dare I say it?)
the man that I put in power
would really like the plot;

but still – it's got hit potential
and if we find an actress
with mutton big enough to steal
the rape scene and dress

there in a scanty transparent
red, well, my friend
then and perhaps only then,
your film could pay your rent."

Left untitled in the ensuing melee (titre provisoire)

Michelle Noteboom

A storm can have little more meaning than trafficking wildly through fields whereas human destiny is to eat on a train. We keep bumping like things that go in the night. Holding back information is empowering though I admit to a burning need to read her. The shed hung exploded in the specially built room and shadowed in the crannies on the wall. First he said there was something synthetic about it and then he made me cry. Feeling slightly like a lackey as of late. I need a new bunny. Loneliness is so photogenic but it doesn't always translate well. I asked for fire and he pulled out a lighter embossed with a purebred basset hound. Now there's a concept. Overheard in a rectangular room full of Rothkos, "It's cool. There's like murders and stuff." A propos de rien, the words dissolve back into ink. Confusion of the non-visual in terms of ruminating utterly basic principles such as brushing your teeth before bed. Who's to blame for the hymen and the heap of cat on the floor? There'll always be some man ready with his corkscrew. We don't do refunds but you can exchange within 30 days upon proof of purchase.

A writer's life

Nessa O'Mahony

I get to the Ferlinghetti part
but my eye keeps drifting
from the print to the tiled floor,
to the powder crystalised around a cigarette-butt,
to the large madame checking the séchoir,
rippling the air as she shakes out sheets
she folds into huge squares.
To my left, the thumping swirl,
a constant spin of towels and underwear.
A black sock becomes for an instant
an agonised L pinned against glass,
then disappears into the vortex.

It's gonna take a lotta love; or, God bless the conspiracy

Richard Peabody

Mars needs women.

China needs oil.

Hey maybe they can work out a deal
For all those unwanted Chinese girl babies?

Big Oil doesn't care about women or children
Or caribou, or Inuit, or gators, or swampland.
Big Oil needs love though, and lots of it.

Do you think they have a contingency plan
Up their sleeves for when the fossil fuels are gone?

I mean besides perpetual alerts and World War III?

Russia needs love.

They have all this untapped oil under the Caspian Sea
And no way to dig it up and no way to distribute it.

Beginning to sound like a James Bond film isn't it?

China needs love.

They have people lining up to get car tags
So they can chase their NASCAR dreams.

And Big Oil needs a lotta love.

Cuz they can drill the oil and pump it through
A new pipeline to the Chinese so they can embrace
All of that lovely cha-ching.

And that's a type of love after all. A love that needs

colossal spin control and a publicity machine.

Only one thing stands in the way of this lovefest –
A Stone Age dinosaur of a country called Afghanistan.

And Afghanistan needs all our love
Like some kind of Asian Neil Young.

Dan Rather was on the BBC the other day
To state that we know less about what our
Government is doing right now than at any
Previous time in our country's history.

That sure makes me feel safe.
Don't you feel safe?

Because corporations need love
And Big Oil needs love, too.
So much love that they're even rewriting old
Sci-fi films – gone are the evil corporations
Waging mock wars in *Roller Ball* or *Robo Cop*.
They prefer it when the public sees other
Countries (or planets) as the bad guys, or the threat.

Return with me now to the 1950s.

Mars needs women.

Almost makes me want to wave a flag.
See how many people I can blind
With the Stars and Stripes.
Cuz while you're distracted
I'm sure going to be up to something.

"Remember the Maine!"

Mars needs women so much easier to handle.

Suicide outboards zooming up Puget Sound,
Crop dusters attacking Yankee Stadium.
Life Magazine World War II
Doomsday scenarios.

Don't believe me? Look it up.

Keep them scared in Kalamazoo,
In Wichita, in Grand Junction.

Mars needs women.

China needs oil.

We were sold out long ago.
And we all need a place to hide.

Pogo had it right:
"We have met the enemy and he is us."

Our blindness makes it so.

Mars needs women and so do I.

John Prine had it right:
"Your Flag Decal Won't Get You into Heaven Any More."

"Jesus don't like killin'
no matter what the reason's for."

Stop the war or giant amœbas will eat you

Richard Peabody

"Just shoot him. The world will applaud you." – Kelina Gotman

Mock Iraq war stories started appearing in printouts that were passed around the entire high school. A handful here. A handful there. Each was only a page or two at best. Each had the heading: *Yellow Rose.* The hard copy ended up wadded in balls, left on floors, stuffed in lockers, or swirled about in the after school breeze. But more and more copies of *Yellow Rose* seemed to be taken seriously, circulated from hand to hand, passed around the community to be discussed over lunch, over coffee. Everybody had a theory but nobody could figure out who was writing them. Nobody had a clue. And so they kept coming, as relentless as the 24/7-war news that threatened to pummel even the most dovish of the doves senseless with violence and veracity. Some students loved the bulletins and sided totally with the parody, with the anti-war sentiments. Other louder voices called for the head of the person brazen enough to try to rewrite history. They were furious and wanted to stop whoever was behind the mock news bulletins by any means necessary.

Yellow Rose #1
Bursts of light illuminated the southern horizon of Dallas, the thunder reverberating in the distance. Then, with method and fury, waves of explosions rolled across the heart of Dallas-Fort Worth tonight, shattering the garrisons of George W Bush's three-decade rule and sending flames and black plumes of smoke into the sky.

In a three-hour blitz that at times brought a new blast every 10 seconds, Chinese PLA forces devastated many of the symbols of Bush's government: a presidential ranch, the baseball stadium in nearby Arlington that once housed his Texas Rangers and a security bunker.

The detonations shook buildings and cracked windows miles from the epicenter of the attacks, and smoke smothered the city in an acrid haze. Soon after the strike began, sirens of emergency vehicles wailed through the deserted, but still-lit streets, although there were no immediate reports on the number of casualties. Texas radio was knocked off the air temporarily.

The assault was by far the most intense since the conflict began Thursday. After two previous air strikes, which both lasted less than an hour, residents had left their barricaded homes stockpiled with food and gingerly returned to the streets. But tonight's attack, beginning shortly after 8pm, and lasting late into the night, was more powerful and wider in scope. The city promptly became a fragile and vacant shell.

Reilly didn't want to die. The idea that a dirty bomb could take out his hometown and kill him and his family was tough to grapple with. His mom was here, his dad in San Francisco. Maybe he should ask them if he could switch coasts? He still had a year of high school to go. Decisions, decisions.

Besides, Reilly thought, all you had to do was make a bomb the size of a cell phone. Security never checked cell phones when he went to a concert or to see the Wizards play ball. They never bothered to look closely. You simply held your cell phone up. Surely this must have occurred to some of the bad guys by now?

English class. Miss Byrne was droning on and on about French history. They were reading Dickens. She'd been at the January 18th march. 500,000 hit the streets around the Capitol steps. It was freezing. 15 degrees. Reilly's toes never did warm up. His Doc Martens no match for the chill. The crowd stunned Reilly.

Surely this would have an impact on the world? When the shoulder-to-shoulder marchers got to the top of the hill by the Library of Congress, he strayed off to the side to rest. It was much too cold to sit on the icy marble so he leaned against a doorway and watched the people keep coming.

And there was Miss Byrne. "Like something out of Dickens ehh Reilly?" It was totally out of context seeing her amid the crowd. They were reading *A Tale of Two Cities*. Reilly found it pretty slow going. He hadn't been paying a lot of attention. He'd been much more interested in the copy of *Infinite Jest* his dad had sent him for his 17th birthday. Still, he waved back and said, "Yeah," though he had no idea what she meant.

Now she was making jokes about Freedom Fries and the ridiculous notion that somebody in Louisiana was putting forth a proposal to change the name of the French Quarter in New Orleans to "Freedom Quarter". None of his other teachers were this cool.

In the first dream Reilly was walking and walking through winding streets. There were hordes of people and they only stopped when they reached a long line outside the Supreme Court. Somehow he had a pass and was led up the steps to the front of the line, and into the courtroom that morphed out larger and larger, into something like the Roman coliseum, until he found himself seated while war criminals were tried. This wasn't anything like the European History Current Events class he'd taken; there was no Milosevic here. In the hot seat were Bush administration folks like Elliot Abrams, Williams Kristol, Condoleezza Rice, Harvey Pitt, Tom DeLay, and radio talk show host Mike Savage.

But the main fixture in the center of the courtroom, which kept shifting back and forth from having a roof to having no roof, was a judge's bench almost two-stories high. Once prisoners were found guilty they were escorted out the back of the building. Curiosity got the best of Reilly and soon he was flying or floating really, outside above the walls and into the courtyard where a noisy crowd of several hundred thousand people had gathered. Every eye was fixed in the center of the courtyard as the prisoners were led up the dais to a gigantic three-story scaffold.

Reilly was watching Canadian TV on C-Span. They were interviewing Iraqi civilians about the recent air strikes and the death toll in greater Baghdad when his cell vibrated in his jeans. He would never admit to feeling a bit of a responsive buzz. "Yeah?" It was Amy. Life was looking up.

"It's you isn't it?"

"Maybe?"

"Don't play coy, Reilly. You're too virginal to work it."

"So? So what?" Could he eat chips and salsa and talk to Amy? She was a cheerleader. She was beautiful. They said hello every day but that was about it. He'd been playing with a solitary chip since he answered the phone. To dip or not to dip? To chew? She was so hot. Did he dare keep eating?

"Don't you think it's a bit much?"

"So's Bush's folly."

"I just don't believe you can repay evil for evil."

"Why not?" He waited, danced the chip across his lips. Tasted the salt. Maybe?

"Cuz you have better things to do with your time? Because you're creative. You can write."

What a trip. This must be how David Foster Wallace felt. Praise. Groupies. What next? Chips? Definitely chips.

"So I want to know."

"Wanna know what?" He plunged the chip into his mouth and the chomping began.

"Why'd you do it?"

Yellow Rose #2

One of the main targets was the Bush ranch complex, which stretches along the west bank of the Trinity river. A faux western town sits at the center of the sprawling complex, built in the 1950s, that houses apartments for some of Bush's loyalists and camps for the Republican Party elite. Missile strikes left at least two buildings in the complex burning, although not the ranch itself. At least five missiles struck the nearby headquarters of Texaco. Even after the attack, the ranch complex remained brightly lit, a lamp casting a ghostly brightness through billowing white smoke.

The Republican Party headquarters was also struck, as was the Heritage Foundation office, a camp on Dallas's southern outskirts where both Republican Party members and regular army units are stationed. Under a full moon, the fires burned for hours and clouds of smoke drifted over downtown Dallas.

Air raid sirens sounded at about 8pm, but the first strikes were visible only as dozens of flashes in the distance. Less than an hour later, the full brunt of the attack struck the heart of

Dallas. For 20 minutes, explosions went off every few seconds. A lull followed, then another round of attacks. That pattern continued until about 11pm.

The strikes appeared to target military installations and symbols of Bush's rule. Electricity remained on in Dallas-Fort Worth throughout the evening, suggesting that the city's fragile and precarious infrastructure had not been targeted. Despite the attack and Chinese advances elsewhere in Texas, the government maintained a confident face and kept control.

Official statements insisted victory was imminent, even as signs of a military defeat grew. In what is becoming a trademark refrain, Information Minister Ari Fleischer heaped insults on China.

"You consider them a superpower. Well, this is a disgrace, a complete disgrace. They are a superpower of villains," he said, dressed in leather chaps and a black Stetson. "Genghis Khan is the typical Beijing official these days."

He denied that Texas had lost any territory today to Chinese forces and insisted that the government retained control of El Paso. He suggested Chinese disinformation was behind reports of the surrender of Texas soldiers in the west.

"We are experienced. We know them very well," Fleischer told reporters. "We know their tricks, their tactics. We know everything about them." Asked whether the government was becoming disheartened, he answered: "Our morale is in us, in our resilience, in our good understanding of the situation, in our deep belief that we are the just side and they are the villains."

Reilly attended his first peace march in October and the world moved. It was awe-inspiring. Giant puppets, amazing signs. The colorful outpouring of humanity. Grannies and infants in Baby Bjorn's. Babies in strollers and old hippies. College professors, students, workers, people of color. He chanted, "This is what democracy looks like" with 200,000 people.

At home later he watched CNN and was dismayed to hear the city officials decry the anti war protests. Saying only 10,000 to 30,000 people had gathered. Who did their math? It was like the polls that claimed 70% of America believed in Bush and the possibility of war. That was impossible. It continued to run against everything Reilly knew to be true. Who was conducting these polls? It sounded rigged to make Bush look good. Too much like the Florida election debacle.

Reilly's email was the usual mix: pleas for money from anti war groups, info from Moveon.org, and Bush cartoons that portrayed the president as either a Nazi or *Mad* magazine's Alfred E Neuman. He also found a new batch of protest pix from the San Francisco march that his dad had sent.

Frodo failed – Bush has the ring
The Only Bush I'd Trust Is My Own (complete with graphic)
Weapons of Mass Distraction
No Blood for Oil
Bombing for Peace is like Fucking for Virginity
Drop Bush Not Bombs

Bichons Against Bush (as in the dog Bichon Frise)
Eat More Pretzels (Motherfucker!)
Appoint an Oil President – Get an Oil War
But Reilly's favorite and the one that almost made him drop his laptop he was laughing so hard was a placard carried by a 10-year-old boy, which read:
Stop the War or Giant Amœbas Will Eat You.
That was the best. Absolutely the best. He'd watched a sorry old sci-fi film called *The Angry Red Planet* with his baby boomer dad. Special effects were almost nonexistent – a solarized giant Martian rat spider was the best thing in the film – but watching the giant amœbæ suck one of the crew into its Jell-O stomach and digest him was hysterical. After that viewing disaster, Reilly had rented the remake of *The Blob* so his dad could see a much more realistic monster digest a ton of people.

Yellow Rose #3

On the second day of the war, scenes in the capital of Austin ranged from the wrenching to the theatrical. Ari Fleischer was joined at his news conference by Colin Powell. Powell wore a flak jacket, to which he had strapped a hunting knife and four ammunition clips, and carried a pistol on his side. To the delight of photographers, he swung a pistol above his head with his finger on the trigger.

"Some of you might wonder why I have a Colt 45 in my hand and why I'm wearing a flak jacket. We have all in Texas pledged never to drop our weapon, to relinquish our weapon, until the day of victory," he said. Powell shouted: "Remember the Alamo!" The mood was far different in the streets of Dallas, a city of almost two million, where residents enjoyed a precarious period of calm in the morning, before the evening's terrifying fusillade. In contrast to previous days in which Dallas was shadowed by an unsettled calm, signs of vibrancy returned in the daylight hours, and residents seemed emboldened that the air strikes Thursday appeared to be restrained by comparison with what many had expected.

"Before the war, the Chinese said they were going to hit us every day with 4,000 missiles, 24 hours a day," said Rabbi Asher Goldstein. "People went home and hid. But what happened is the opposite. Thank God, praise be to God."

Savannah, Reilly's kid sister, kept a candlelight vigil on their front porch. Every morning he was amazed: one, that there house hadn't burned down in the night; and two, at the spooky-looking piles of wax. Last night when he got home there was a tiny Pooh lamp plugged into an extension cord that fed under the storm door. His mom had been worried about the candles.
"Do you have any idea how expensive candles are?" she said. His mom was making a batch of power pancakes – cottage cheese added to the mix. "Oh, did you see my sign?"
"What sign?"
"Look," she said, and she led him to the window getting batter on his ear, and

pointed in the front yard. How had he missed it in the dark?

"War Is Not the Answer." Blue words on a white background.

"Where did you get it?"

"The Quakers. Which reminds me..."

"What?"

"When are you going to do something to get this warmonger out of the White House?"

"I marched." If she only knew the truth, Reilly thought.

"Yeah, well that was a few weeks ago. What have you done for me lately?"

"C'mon, mom, gimme a break."

"Yeah? Well, you're a smart kid. You can do something else. I'm sure you will. And oh. That reminds me. Have you seen this?"

Reilly's jaw dropped open. His mom pushed a copy of *Yellow Rose* across the counter to him. Butter had stained one corner.

"Err, no. What is it?" Did his voice betray him?

"The sound of one voice crying in the wilderness. I found it on a table at Whole Foods this morning. Now Reilly dear, you could do something like this. Become a pamphleteer. I want you to take it and read it."

"Sure mom." Reilly took it to his room. Plopped it on a pile in his drawer of about 200 more copies.

Dream voices keep the count. Reilly is back in the courtyard watching the crowd chant: "Twenty-two. Twenty-two." The rich, the fat cats, are led to where mistress guillotine presides, led like sheep for shearing. A pretty head is held aloft by long blonde hair. Ann Coulter. Laughter ripples through the crowd. CEOs and chairmen. Suits. Extravagant Italian suits. All pomp and circuitous lies within the spirit of the law. Laws invented by the rich, for the rich, and nobody but the rich. And yet we knit and count "Twenty-three. Twenty-three." Why not 203? 2003? Mistress guillotine is rapacious. She'll lick you and kiss you and drink your blood. She has a real appetite for skin.

Here comes Karen Hughes. Richard Perle. Now Cheney. His wife talking, beseeching. Snicker-snak. Heads roll. Drop into the basket, the blood seeping through the weave. Now Newt. Now Rush. Sardonic masks. They came, they saw, they got down on their knees and revealed their lily-white necklines to the silver glint. The law of gravity. That shuddering fall of steel rimmed with bloody splatter.

Yellow Rose #4

While spectacular high-tech air strikes in Dallas captured the world's attention, what was happening in the rest of Texas yesterday revealed a more aggressive, even daring, side of today's Chinese military.

Special Operations troops, taking a far more important role in the invasion than they did during the war in Tibet, seized an airfield and other key points in the western desert, making it much less likely that Texas will be able to use Minuteman or Cruise missile launching pads to strike back. In the north, a smaller force of Special Operations troops worked near Amarillo and Lubbock to create a northern front.

Most significantly, from the south, several columns of armored troops drove deep into Texas, racing more than 10 miles toward Austin.

"Reilly, Reilly. Get out of bed. Somebody stole my sign. They stole my peace sign right out of our yard.

"Mom, it's okay. That's happening all over. We'll just get another one."

"But you don't know how long it took to get that one. I was on the phone forever and finally I just drove down to the Quaker meeting house at Dupont Circle and picked one up."

"It'll be okay."

"God I hate whoever did that."

"Ashcroft."

"What?"

"I'll bet Ashcroft drives around in a long black stretch limo late at night with a team of sign ripper uppers."

His mom laughed. Reilly always liked the way she laughed. Her entire face wrinkled up. It was kind of Meg Ryanish squinty eyed. Nothing like Julia Roberts and her toothy hyena head rolls. No, making mom laugh always made Reilly feel warm and fuzzy. Something he hadn't seen enough of since the divorce. Reason enough to go on living.

Yellow Rose #5

A column of 100 to 150 Texas tanks broke out of the besieged city of Houston tonight as Chinese troops continued to barrage Texans with artillery fire, Chinese military officials said.

A day after Chinese military officials declared Enron positions inside Houston a legitimate military target and prepared to enter the city, it was still unclear there was a civilian uprising against the rule of President George W Bush, as Chinese officials reported Tuesday.

The fighting moved outside of Houston tonight as the column of tanks poured out of the city and headed southeast toward Galveston and the Gulf of Mexico. The tanks were immediately pounded by Chinese aircraft. The attack continued late into the night.

Reilly could taste blood. His face was skinned from where he'd slid across the blacktop. Somebody had slammed him hard.

"Rumor has it that you're the little dickhead who writes this Texas crap."

Bruno. Death metal drummer. He of the bald head and black leather. People were beginning to gather. Reilly managed to pull himself up to a knee; the damage didn't feel too awful. He could live with it. But fighting Bruno was suicide.

"Who says?"

"It's you. You know it. I know it. They all know it."

"So? Don't you believe in Freedom of Speech?"

"Not when my brother's in Kuwait. Not when some little ass wipe is writing treason."

"Treason?"

"That's right. Now get up." This was delivered with menacing fingers."First I'm going to make you eat this crap," he said, rolling a copy of *Yellow Rose* into a tight wand, "and then I'm gonna beat the fuck out of your faggot ass self."

And then somebody pushed Bruno from behind. "What the?"

It was Rafael. Rafael Ramirez. Nose guard on the football team. His green and orange Miami football jersey blocking out the sun. This was more like it. A battle of behemoths.

"I've got no beef with you, Rafael. This is between me and dickhead here."

"You don't get it, Bruno? I'd rather fight Republicans than eat."

"Some pacifist."

"Since when do you have to be a pacifist to be against the war?"

"You guys are both traitors."

"You know, the Pope says this war is a sin. That's good enough for a good Catholic boy like me."

"My brother's over there."

"I'm sorry, vato. I hope they bring him home. But I don't buy that America right or wrong crap."

The executioners in the dream are masked. One mans the long nylon rope that starts the blade in motion. The other has the more gruesome chore of hoisting heads for the crowd's reaction, then clearing the cadavers from their position, before heaving them below to the waiting cart. The stack of bodies is getting impressively high. Crows have appeared. For some reason Cypress Hill is playing on a stage in the square.

Here comes Wolfowitz. Karl Rove. Whomp. Whomp. Heads roll. Blood flies high. Legs twitch and jerk. The crowd roars. Tom Ridge is next. Then William J Bennett. The mob wants to build a tower of Republican dead. Yet they save one of the biggest roars for Ashcroft. One executioner must sit on Ashcroft's legs to keep him pinned in place for his close shave.

"It was an experiment. I wanted to see what would happen if you changed a few words around. That's the original idea any way."

"Really?"

"Yep. But the thing started growing out of control."

Reilly thought of the bagpiper. There's an instrument you could never play in a group house, or an apartment. Like a tuba. The guy was playing the bagpipes out in the middle the grassy knoll between two lanes of the E Street Expressway. Obviously a George Washington student. Practicing to the morning rush hour. Reilly had wanted to come back at dusk after the march to see if the bagpiper was still there.

"Look, I'm trying to decide if I want to help you or not. I need to know that you're doing this because you believe you're doing the right thing. That it's not just some pointless intellectual exercise."

Reilly must have misheard. Did cheerleader Amy just say what he thought she'd said?

"I'm serious Reilly. I want to help. I think this is an awesome thing you're doing. Forcing people to wear the other shoe."

Reilly wasn't sure that was what he was doing. He was just playing with words. In some ways it was only a game. In others he knew he was becoming more and more emotional about the war. The inevitable civilian casualties. And he was perturbed by the smoke screen military jargon: friendly fire, collateral damage, embedded correspondents, et al.

"Well, Amy, what do you say we go see Michael Moore's *Bowling for Columbine*?"

Yellow Rose #6

"Love your enemies" – Jesus

Only one member of Congress has a child serving in Iraq.

Seventy per cent of members of Congress do not own passports. Because they never intend to leave this country. Why would you want to after all? America has everything, right?

None of Bush's administration has served in the military during wartime save Colin Powell and Donald Rumsfeld.

Banditry and lawlessness appear to be spreading through some areas in southwestern Texas as Chinese troops sweep the countryside for remnants of Texas forces and remain at a stalemate with fighters in Houston, Texas's largest city.

Villagers in the area now complain of roving bands of armed men who steal tractors, hijack trucks, loot factories and terrorize residents with near impunity.

At the same time, Texas paramilitary fighters of the Charlton Heston Brigade inside Houston fired mortars and machine guns today on about 1,000 civilians trying to leave the besieged city, forcing them to retreat.

Amy joined Reilly at the March 15th peace rally. There weren't as many people but it was a lot warmer and everything was beautiful until they made the turn onto Pennsylvania Avenue and into the teeth of the pro-war rally. He'd heard right-wingers argue that the peace marchers were all communists, but when the odd mix of white bread Republicans and vets began shouting at them he thought it was hilarious. Save for the hatred. The US was so totally half and half on every subject that it was getting to be like the Balkans. "Don't they realize that Castro is the last communist?"

"It's hysterical."

"Except that they'd like to kill us."

Their walk back to the Washington Monument was very sobering. They grabbed some coffee at Starbucks and took the Metro back home to Virginia. About the time students were getting off at Foggy Bottom, Amy repeated her offer, "I want to help."

"Help what?"

"Don't be stupid, Reilly. I know it's you. Let me help. I can do the graphics.Spruce up your typefaces. Help you hand them out at the next peace march."

Yellow Rose #7

Swiftly moving columns of Chinese tanks and armored vehicles pushed halfway to Dallas today as Chinese forces farther south tightened their grip on Houston, Texas, and allied warplanes and ships rained bombs and missiles on the Texas capital in a day-and-night pounding.

The fast-paced Chinese invasion prompted hundreds of Texans to surrender and thousands of others to shed their uniforms and head home, said General Qiao Chang, the overall commander of Chinese forces in Texas, who boasted in a briefing that the military campaign will be "unlike any other in history." The Army's 38th Infantry Division, which has been barreling through the desert in southwestern Texas with tanks and fighting vehicles since Thursday, had pierced 150 miles into Texas by nightfall – about half the distance between the Mexican border and Dallas, Chinese military officials said. Army sources said the division's lead elements, moving on during the night, clashed with Texas troops 45 miles southeast of Midland, a city that is important to Bush and the oil industry.

"Do you think any of these people have kids?"

"Bush has the twins."

"Besides them?"

"You want to know what I think?"

"Shoot."

"I think most of the Bush administration isn't really human. I think they're demons disguised in flesh. Reptilian invaders from the demon realm."

"You've got to stop watching *Lord of the Rings* – today."

"Can I ask you something?"

"Sure." Now what? Reilly was worried.

"Why China?"

"What?"

"I mean why did you choose them? Why my people?"

Reilly hadn't made the connection. The Chinese just seemed like the obvious aggressors in a piece like this, a piece that would hold a mirror up to what the USA was doing to the Muslim world. But he said, "Mexico seemed too unbelievable and Canada was too *South Park*."

"You know I'm Chinese."

"Yeah, of course."

"Amy's my adopted name."

"Okay."

"My real name is Zhen."

"Jun? Like fun? What's it mean?"

"Precious."

"Wow."

"Reilly, I want you to call me Zhen from now on."

Yellow Rose #8

Units of the 38th Infantry Division barreled deeper into Texas in several columns, one of which encountered resistance from Texas fighters near College Station. But other columns of the 40th Infantry Division speeding through the desert farther to the west, met no resistance as they pushed toward rendezvous points en route to the Texas capital of Austin."We will try to force the Bush regime to capitulate as quickly as possible with minimum damage to civilians, the Chinese military spokesman told reporters. "There is not a desire to destroy Texas. What we are going to do is liberate Texas from a dictator."

Reilly listened to The Flaming Lips on the Jeep's CD player. He was parked in front of the library. A slow moving light in the sky distracted him and then as it proved to be a small plane he found himself pondering that if the aliens were so smart why were they always taking farmers and cowhands and lonely women driving cross-country? Why didn't they just come down to Earth right this second and snatch Bush and Cheney and Rumsfeld and Ashcroft. And hell yes, take Saddam, too. Nobody ever said Saddam was a good guy. Just take the lot of them off and give them the anal probe for a couple of decades. The world would be at peace by day's end.

The door opened and Zhen piled into the front seat. "Go, go, go, go," she said breathless. Laughing, as the door slammed.

"So your idea of helping is what? Getting us arrested for defacing public property?"

"Oh Reilly, you're so lame. You do this great thing and you don't want people to read it."

"At the library?"

"At the library, on the library. Any and everywhere." Zhen was taping copies of *Yellow Rose* on doors, walls, staple-gunning others to telephone poles.

Reilly had to admit that Zhen's new design was spectacular. She'd added desk-topped maps of Texas with the invasion almost totally paralleling the US invasion of Iraq. She printed it out on her father's law firm's super duper color printer and the results were very zippy and made early attempts look naïve. Now here she was helping him distribute them. The initial print-run of 300 copies for *Yellow Rose #1* was now dwarfed by the free printing possibilities Zhen could gather at her father's office. They had 3,000 copies to unload now. So why, since he was rubbing elbows with Zhen, and staring at her immaculate face for hours daily, why, did he feel like it was time to quit?

Yellow Rose #9

Commanders declared that Galveston, the port city on the Gulf of Mexico, was secure. Chinese officials now face the logistics challenge of housing prisoners of war. As of this morning, the Chinese military said it had taken 8,900 prisoners, about 4,000 of them by the Commandos.

Reilly waits at Teaism at Dupont Circle for Zhen to show up. It's Saturday and they're having sushi. He's totally dismayed when Rafael slides onto a bench beside her.

"What's up?" Rafael says.

"Hey." Reilly looks to Zhen for guidance and finding none he studies his menu.

"Rafael knows," Zhen says.

"Knows what?" Reilly says.

"C'mon, vato, I knew it was you ever since Bruno came after you. I think it's great what you're doing."

Reilly makes as if to go, to stand, but Zhen puts a hand on his arm. "Please Reilly, hear him out. He really wants to help."

"I've got a thou saved up. My brother and I always play slots once a year at Atlantic City and we made a killing last weekend. I'll give it all to you for this thing you're doing. No strings."

"We can print 5,000 copies per issue," Zhen says. Her smile is big enough to get lost in.

Yellow Rose #10

Screams echoed throughout the Red Cross hospital. Two Texas women lay bleeding with shrapnel wounds in their arms and legs. A row over a dead woman, another, two women sobbing, the sisters of one of the women. Their husbands and brothers bodies lying dead outside. The dead children.

"The Chinese did it," said an angry Texan from the crowd of onlookers. "They shot us down like dogs." The Chinese military doctor who dressed their wounds had no idea what had transpired. "Civilian casualties have been light up to now," he said. "They come with the territory."

Zhen is loudly delivering a monologue to Reilly and anybody else in earshot in the school cafeteria. "They haven't found any weapons of mass destruction. Iraq has no air force. They've fired what? 6 missiles since the war started? The US fighting Iraq is like Mike Tyson in the ring with an infant."

Reilly can feel his cell phone vibrating. He takes a look. It's mom.

"Dear, can you come home? Right now?"

"Sure, mom. What's wrong?"

"Savannah had a run-in with the sign ripper uppers."

"What?"

"Just come home."

Zhen runs after him to the Jeep and they haul back to Reilly's house. It's only a few blocks away.

"Why didn't you go to high school at Woodlawn?" she asks him as they drive past the other nearby high school campus. The boho artsy students sunning themselves by the front drive.

"Huh?"

"Never mind. Why didn't I go to Woodlawn?"

There's an Arlington County policeman in the yard talking to his mom. She has her arms across her chest. Savannah is nowhere to be seen. As Reilly and Zhen walk up, the policeman looks them over and returns to his white car.

"What's going on?" Reilly says.

Reilly is enveloped in a bear hug. Embarrassed, he manages to gasp, "Mom, this is Zhen."

"Oh hi," his mom releases him and wipes a tear. And then much to Reilly's shock his mom and Zhen hug.

"Savannah's inside. Mrs Novak is eating Popsicles with her. She'll be fine. She was playing jump rope on the sidewalk when a car stopped out front and some kid hopped the fence to steal my sign. Savannah yelled and the baldheaded kid ran over her, knocked her flat. I'm afraid she got a pair of bloody knees and a boo-boo head, but she'll be okay. I'm not sure if I'll survive though."

"Did you say baldheaded?" Zhen asked.

Later, after dinner, after Savannah's gone to bed, Reilly's mom knocks on her son's aluminum foil wrapped door.

"She's cute."

"Zhen?"

"Yes. Is she helping you with *Yellow Rose*?"

"How long have you known?"

"You gave it away over pancakes. Besides, you always print in Garamond."

"You're not mad?"

"I'm proud of you. But I realize a lot of people are going to get pretty steamed about this. I'd hate for you to get hurt."

"Mom?"

"Yes, honey?"

"I'm thinking about quitting."

"Cuz of today?"

"It just feels like we're not allowed to protest what the government is doing. Even the *Washington Post* is supporting the war."

"Well, the hell with them. I'll cancel our subscription tomorrow. We can't afford the daily *NY Times* but I think we have enough for the Sunday edition. Good enough?"

"Thanks, mom."

"And Reilly."

"Yeah?"

"If you want to quit doing *Yellow Rose* that's okay, too."

Yellow Rose #11

In the west, Mexican troops have joined their Chinese allies. Armored columns are streaming across the Mexican border at Brownsville and Laredo and are converging on San Antonio. The Mexican forces have met little resistance from Texas forces thus far. Additional Mexican forces have taken over the occupation of El Paso freeing Chinese troops for the push on to Austin and Dallas-Fort Worth.

Now that Rafael is part of the team he suggests some changes.

"Mexico is Turkey, see."

"What?"

"Turkey wouldn't allow us to invade from their border with Iraq but now I'm going to make Mexico join in. That Alamo quote inspired me."

Reilly felt sluggish. Was he really tired or simply tired of maintaining his big secret?

"Look Rafael, I think I'm going to bag out."

"What? You can't bag this was your idea."

"I had my fun. I got my point across. Right now I'm pretty depressed by how helpless I feel about this country."

"But vato, you're doing something. You're doing something real..."

Zhen came around the corner with a very long face.

"What's up, girlfriend?" Rafael asked.

"Bruno's brother died. On one of the choppers."

Rafael put an arm around Zhen. She had tears in her eyes. Reilly felt empty. *Yellow Rose* wasn't real like this. Dying was real.

"That's it then," Reilly said, "I'm done."

Yellow Rose #12

Houston is still under siege. Texas army regulars and members of Bush's Davy Crockett and Jessie Helms militia groups have interspersed themselves among civilians, leaving Chinese com-

mandos wondering aloud whether they will have to enter the city and face house-to-house combat with hardcore fighters.

After short-lived Texan resistance, the Mexican 2nd Infantry Division column seized the city of San Antonio, along with two bridges traversing Cibolo Creek, opening a route for thrusts toward Austin on both sides of the waterway, the officials said. The other column raced farther west, pausing to battle pockets of Texas defenders before pushing on in the direction of San Angelo.

At school the next day, Reilly felt sad and just as depressed by world events but freed up somehow. Less paranoid. More relaxed. He'd stayed up most of the night finishing *A Tale of Two Cities*. Now his dreams made more sense. Like he was remembering the future in some weird time bendable way.

Zhen found him already sitting in his English class. Today was the big Dickens test. She handed him the latest installment of *Yellow Rose*. There was a great map with big red troop arrows splashing across the Mexican border.

"So, what do you think?"

"Feels kind of nice to have something live on after you're through working on it," Reilly began.

"I'm not going to help Rafael with the next installment. I respect your opting out too much to continue. But..."

"But what?" Reilly watched Zhen's eyes. She glanced away and then quickly back. Her eyes were a warm brown, so brown.

"I hope you'll use that amazing brain of yours to come up with something else to show your love for the world."

"That's what my mom says."

"I am most definitely not your mom," Zhen said, and then leaned over and gave him a kiss on the cheek. Before Reilly could respond she'd breezed out of the room.

Miss Byrne placed a copy of the English test in Reilly's upraised right hand like she was passing him a baton. "Okay, lover boy, time to get to work." And then she chuckled. "You know, Reilly, if we survive this war it'll take 50 years to fix the damage this administration has done to the country. You'll have lots of time to make it better."

Reilly smiled. The splendiferous Zhen had kissed him. Time stopped. And then he put the test down and read the first several questions.

1 How far would you go to obtain revenge on someone or some group who destroyed your family?

2 Can you achieve justice through revenge?

3 What is justice?

4 How does our society treat those who achieve revenge?

Compared to secretly doing *Yellow Rose* and worrying constantly about getting in trouble this test was going to be a breeze.

The bloodthirsty dream crowd has almost grown weary of the endless parade of Republicans. There's a certain sameness to the routine by now. Another key Reagan or Papa Bush crony or henchman is brought out to the dais and beheaded with numbing regularity. There are the occasional flourishes to spice things up – Columnist George Will asks for a blindfold; Kathleen Harris claims *she's pregnant* and pleads for her life. Reilly finds it amusing that she'd use the *Chicago* defense. The crowd is not amused. They have long memories. Of course G Gordon Liddy makes a grab for a gun, only to be wrestled to the ground. He dies weeping. But make no mistake – a druggy sort of tedium has set in. People are starting to get drunk, bored, unruly. And then in the gathering gloom anticipation ignites the crowd when it realizes there are only a few key figures that remain. And as George W Bush is led out into the courtyard the cameras of the paparazzi ignite the lazy Washington, DC honeysuckle night with explosive pops and flashes, enough to momentarily resemble the anti-aircraft fireworks in the sky over Baghdad. Seconds later the nightmare is over.

Burning Omaha

Tom Phillips

All summer it was like a miracle,
the dust coating cars and running
your finger through sand they said
had blown in from the Sahara.
Drivers cursed. It was the summer, too,
of talk about incidents, evacuation,
populations gridlocking ring roads,
four-minute warnings, the hottest season
of the Cold War. We didn't care.
We were racing through the woods
while parents stocked up on tins
and candles or stared at the radio
with palms against their throats
as if by suddenly tightening their grip
they could hold their little faith in.
There was no rain, only sand,
only sand coming down like scurf,
like unexpected snow from Archangel,
like the ashes from Omaha burning.

kyoto crow(s)

David Prater

we are many we are one kyoto
crow(s) built by basho wings a
trigger or a swoop the fantailed
roof shine beak(s) crow patrol
command high rises the entire
dim days plans collapse spare
flight paths then or red clouds
glitter rush released the night
reconstructs an atoms dresses
end weaves miniature cranes
down on impossible street as
daylight narcotic canals paper
plates announce new vending
machines advancing mornings
jettisoned our bansai awnings
the day shines smoking "lark"

Kernel

Sina Queyras

"Nature is dead," the business major says, "there's no point
trying to *connect* with it." He tugs on the strap of his sixteen
pocket, triple construction pack with built in water-bottle and cell
phone slots. "I mean what's the point now?" The microfibres
of his plum, polar-tec jacket rubbing against canvas fills
the bare office with a cricketing song. A curled maple leaf
see-saws through the open window between us, lands
on my hush-puppied toe. "Why not take the money and run?"
His dark eyes narrow and moisten: "Shouldn't we be realistic?
Why try to resuscitate the past when we can re-create it, cleaner,
more efficiently, providing new opportunities for growth?"
He shifts his weight, laughs, "I mean, I saw the Green platform:
what good is raising the minimum wage?" He bobs nervously,
unsure of what he wants, of why he is here, his featherless
heart a newly discovered reptilian bird. Despite himself
he leans in, urgently, fingers fluttering the edge of the wooden
desk, cuff of his jeans, plastic arm of the chair, his enormous,
intelligent head worrying the small kernel of doubt into his ribcage
as he searches for affirmation, diagnosis in the autumn air,
as if deep inside him he knows he has only moments
before the body absorbs that kernel of doubt, begins layering it,
hardening, and benign or not, it begins to grow.

Carthage

Srikanth Reddy

Moonlight flecks a wasp's husk in the rainbarrel.
You can't see through to the bottom yet.

Here & there, frail bubbles ferry the odor
of resin to the rim. She rolls up her sleeves

& reaches in. Heat sleeves her to the elbow
then spills over the edge, waking the dreaming lizard

coiled at the base. Elsewhere, chained horses
strain to extract a fuselage from the field,

white noise skittering through headsets
in the burnt-out cockpit. The baby comes out

heavy & clean. She sets him down in the basket –
in her head, a song she once heard along

the footpath, sung by a man planting his shovel
in ash. The end of the song was just

the song's beginning. It goes round. It goes
moonlight flecks a wasp's husk in the rainbarrel...

"If you think they don't go crazy in tiny rooms"

Ali Riley

He left a star-shaped stain in the middle of the Motel 6 floor.
So much for *that* party trick, she thinks.
She came in here eight days ago to vacuum,
now she languishes like Catherine Deneuve in *Repulsion*.
He's taken to hiding
piles of powder for her to find,
powder she's afraid to try.
Would it rev her up or slow her down?
Where is he anyway?
Has it really been over a week?
Her beige maid's dress, not quite a colour,
more like all flavours of boredom
melted into one sad shade.
Not a pinch of interest to this outfit,
but for the tiny speck of chipped nail polish
(Scarlet pimpernel)
nestled in the waffle-weave.

These are deluxe accomodations,
but she's still not sure why she's here.
She recieved a stack of tens on the bedside table two days ago
but since then nothing but the star.
This stain.

"Stella" she says out loud, looking at it.
The air conditioner sighs along with her,
feel, see, whisper, listen, it says.
soar however you can extolls the bar fridge,
its pitch rising,
it adopts a wheedling tone –
soar you must!
with brandy, with words, with gracefull appetite-
she finally unplugs it.
she finds a plastic sign hanging from the dooknob.
"Maid – please make this room sing with your spirit"
and on the other side, simply

"Please be profound".
This melanine and Fortrel won't yet help her transcend,
but they ache to be used
to climb to heaven.
All things, even the pock-marked
mystery-stained upolstery.
of a motel chair
(especially that!)
beg to be used for something other than
dull, vile practices.

Direct your attention to this burn
on the couch. See where the fabric
melts into beads?
This is where the Voice will speak
two days from now.

In her wilder days
she thoughtlessly rolled
joints in the parchment
of Gideon's Bible.
Leaves of Grass!
In the words of G-d!
Suddenly this horrifies her.

What emmisary will speak to her
in this place
anonymous as an airport
neither here nor there?

She will be suddenly silent.
She will mute the Nashville Network
and stare down the grate in the wall.
She will wail,
she will discover her purpose
on this neutral ground.

She will put her head down
she will hear the rustle
hear it settle
she will feel herself to be alone
then she will
be.

A cold room in Granada

Peter Riley

A voice calling in English under the trees
of the square, already they are
going for their newspapers
and she has arrived safely.
The news ends where the story begins.

Now we shall dress our minds
in all the hope of the story
the hill covered in white houses
the long story, the carefully turned
corner of alabaster holding a piece of light

The measuring wheel, carefully turned,
the electric fire hung on a coat-hook,
the water as it flows over the sculpterd edge
agreement between people/s
the trees at night full of birds.

Chattering heart, turn finally
to the end of the story in clear cold light:
the moment achieved, snow on marble,
people living in caves, singing
bodies fruit and die.

Facing death

Peter Robinson

Death's a bit of a yob
who jostles you in the street;
staggering from some pub,
he has to pick a fight.

Past midnight, on hard shoulder,
you're running for dear life.
"Want to get any older?"
asks Death with gun or knife.

Perhaps he's a sorry loner,
or the guru of some cult;
still, you're dead and gone for
not pocketing an insult.

What is Death afraid of
that he needs to compensate?
Not seeming tough enough?
"One day," he says, "you wait!"

No, there's not much comical
about how we have to die;
perhaps for no reason at all,
for a look in the eye

or words I said, but twice...
three times... it's happened now.
Death's cuffed me in the face,
then turned and let me go.

a bed between summer and fall

Noel Rooney

out of the ordinary, there's just us, and spring
bellies into fashion in a playful waistcoat.
its manners are intense. its loveliness
is a prediction, a mythic reciprocal kiss
to name the lovers by, to still and glitter in
your beauty, making things by reading them

gentle breeze, beauty like the night. no one
feels nostalgia like we do – it shines,
our cursory diamond in our central heat
like ice, and we know better than our souls
the soft tattoo of a capable heart, the slim
possibiiity. it will be sweet. it won't be here

Listen up

Thaddeus Rutkowski

Her fingers invade the keyboard while I'm typing. She finds one key and holds it down so that the corresponding character – in this case, an empty square – repeats across the screen. When I pull her hand away and pick her up by the waist and set her on my knee, she waves her arms as if flying. I continue typing with one hand – one finger, actually – because I'm using my other arm to restrain her. Blocked from the keyboard, she reaches for the pen cup. She pulls writing tools from the holder, along with a graphics knife. "No! Not the knife!" I say, then realize I've made a no-no. I've said the word "no," instead of telling her in a positive way what she should do. So I say, "Please leave the keyboard alone, please return the pens to the cup and please avoid the knife." But instead of answering or complying, she waves her hand at me and says, "Bye-bye!" So I switch my approach. I show her how to clip a pencil between her ear and her skull, and I go back to typing. But the next thing I see is, she's sticking the pencil point into her ear. (I've been freaked about her hearing from the time she was a fetus. I worried when she went to a rock concert in the amniotic sac.) So I forget the no-negativity rule and say, "Holy heck! What are you doing? Do you want to puncture your eardrum? Are you trying to put a kink in your Eustachian tube? Do you care if you smash your stirrup and anvil? Don't do that!" She takes the pencil out of her ear, but when I turn back to the computer screen, I've completely forgotten what it is I'm typing about.

Apache tears

Rebecca Seiferle

In the rock bins of my childhood, every tourist stop
sold Apache tears – obsidian drops, smooth and velvety
in the hand, obdurate, until, held up to the light,
then each became a smoky being, a cloud pregnant
with rain in that desert – with the story of the beauty
of grief, a tribe of Apache (really no more than
an extended family) who were trapped at the edge
of the cliff, by the Mexicans some said, others
the US calvary, who all leapt to their deaths
rather than being taken captive, and the tears
they shed before dying turned to wild stones
at the base of the cliff. I don't know how many
tears I bought and lost; a galaxy of darkness
in those bins, and yet each time, I looked through
that landside of sorrow, thinking if I found
the right one and held it up to the light,
I could see entirely through it. If it's ever possible
to see through human suffering: beyond knowing
in any climate and any time, there are those who are turned to stone.

The decline of the beetle empire

John W Sexton

The beetle followed a jagged, hesitant route
through the shifting fingers of grass-shadows,
detoured under the immobile shadows of stones.
        Other shadows, unsubstantial, the fast-moving orbs
of feathered seeds, dandelions, hawkweeds,
brushed swiftly over his path.
        Ants pondered in their mathematical courses
as he trundled past them,
ignoring his polished, resplendent body.
        But then a shadow that appeared suddenly
was no longer a shadow, but the piercing sword
of a shrike's beak. And this swift mouth ended,
with one hammering snap,
the secret knowledge of the Beetle Emperor.
        And there was the Beetle Emperor now,
his black cloak crushed,
his delicate petticoats of wings sliced and torn,
and the index of his incredible mind
scattered everywhere.
        A glistening grass-lizard that had observed
all of this
blinked liquidly,
then disappeared as fast as thought,
the long stalks of grass trembling, trembling
where he had been.
        Underneath the ground worms moved blindly
in their tunnels, siphoning the earth
through their long bodies.
        Nearer to the surface, the larvæ of beetles
also turned in their gritty womb,
and the tendrils of grass roots
felt their way into the darkness,
grain of earth by grain of earth.

Dadaquest

Ron Silliman

Disconnect the dots!
Undifferentiated
beep beep beep
of airport terminal
transport vehicle
The expansion of genre
at a rate much faster
than the expansion
of readers   Blimp
in the shape of
Everready bunny
The sadness of flowers
before frost disproved
Page as original
flat screen display
Slowly, a boy
nods into wakefulness
Auto-ethnography
of rainfall
Cellophane prophecy
Green goose poop
Ducks echoing
up from the quarry
Woodpecker hops
up the bare oak
Yellow jeep
honks to say hi
You have mail
The forest in winter
Pubic hair caught
between two teeth
The trash men come
before the dark fades
day no more
than the night bleached gray
The interpretation

of creams
An old man
with sores bleeding
green-yellow
about the ankles
Linoleum pattern
foretells present
Like pilots
donning parachutes
friends drop away
until only you remain
to guide the plane
the instrumentation panel
entirely unintelligible
Posthumous years
Distant sound
of a train
Woman explains
to the court
that she saw
her boyfriend
beat her daughter
eight years old
who had tried
to keep them from fighting
saw him break both arms
tape her mouth her nose
with duct tape
until the girl went limp
then blue
and did nothing
Cartoon pilgrims
on a flag
decorate suburban porch
Cat with bandaged paw
falls from kitchen table
Two ambulances one fire truck
one paramedic sport utility vehicle
surround the car spun around
into concrete barrier
On the television

football game with the sound off
World in which Strom Thurmond
outlives Kathy Acker
We walk under the grey sky
past the massive brick apartments
of outer Connecticut Avenue
toward a strip mall café
is branded – Ben Gay
The old dental bill
bait-and-switch
Not as a vessel
but against which to struggle
Poem of laughter
become a form of grieving
Lung's cough
defines a margin
The next storm
will surely bring snow

Taking your fun while you can

Hal Sirowitz

Life is supposed to be fun
when you're a kid, Father said.
As you get to be an adult
it becomes hard work. I only
act like I'm having fun
when I'm with my family,
so your mother won't yell at me.
If you expect to wait until you
get older to have fun you might
become deeply disappointed.
When you reach my age
the only fun you'll have is remembering it.

Eight forty five am

Hank Starrs

we walk across the first field
every other day
so many magpies!
we thought they came in pairs
mating for life

he quizzes me
– geography
how long would it take to drive to australia
in a milk float?
or perhaps
– literature
who's best
spiderman or batman?

reaching a gap in the hedge
the second field covered
a quilt of tiny spider webs
allover

he starts a trot
a beat
then top speed
in a second a pale blob
at the black gates
still familiar
he checks and gives a tiny wave
to reassure me

The sacrifice

Sean Street

In memory of Andrei Tarkovsky
"There is no remembrance of former things. Neither shall there be any remembrance of things
that are to come with those that shall come after." – Ecclesiastes
"Nato planes have accidentally bombed a hospital." – News broadcast, May 1999

I

In spite of ourselves we return to the same place
simply because we cannot recall ourselves
ever to have been there before. If we did
we would not come back again.
It is why things always end in the same way.

II

I blow a speck of dust from my hand.
I watch it drift, tiny – so tiny – up.
It seems to hang for a moment then gently
it falls, slowly, softly through the late night
onto the table. Silent. Infinitely delicate.

At the same instant somewhere brute bombs
blast into bone and blood through stone and tin.
Surgical air-strikes. Surgical. Missiles
like space-ships into children.
Why are they hurting me? Have I not been good?

III

Listen. Nothing. It is only the night
beating in my ears. I had thought for a moment
I heard crying. I thought I heard
something strange above me coming closer.
It is nothing. Only the house around me.
Only my children sleeping.

IV

Bombs into blood and bone. What a way
to celebrate Christ. What a way

to cross a threshold, to mark a millennium,
to close or open a door, to punctuate time.
But then again, why not?

V

Cancer and I are old friends.
He has spoken to me often through the eyes
of the people who made me. An old friend.
He's welcome, but like all guests
there's an etiquette to be observed; to be polite
he should know his time. Mostly he does, he understands.
And given that, he's a gentleman. He leaves time
to organise things. He's civilised.
He's not a bomb.

VI

Thank you god of future times for the gift
of forgetfulness. Why would I want to remember this?

VII

What is a gift if it is not a sacrifice?
If a gift has not entailed a sacrifice
how can it be a gift?
            What is it worth?

The waxwing slain

Seamus Sweeney

Traffic had been light, so running into a string of cars at the Goatstown crossroads was disappointing. I was driving against the main bulk of traffic coming away from Dublin, which had built up quite considerably – at least my line is small, I thought, as I looked at the solid mass of unmoving cars beside me, travelling in the other direction. It was High Summer, one of those days when the sun almost nauseates with a rancid, piercing light. Both my windows rolled down all the way, the airconditioning set to the highest setting – despite all this, the smell of melting plastic persisted.

As I eased into the end of the line of cars, indicating right for Stillorgan, I heard a strange sound which, nevertheless, nagged at the edge of familiarity. It took a moment to realise what it was. It was my own voice, reciting the poem which I had published a few months before, The Waxwing Slain. I must explain that this poem was not entirely my own work, though we'll come to that later.

My voice was coming from about six or seven car stereo systems scattered among the line of traffic to my right. All the cars driving in the opposite direction also had their windows down. With recordings of The Waxwing Slain being played on stereos scattered at various points in the block of traffic, a kind of polyphonic speaker relay was set up. Each listener was at a different stage in the poem, though all were within a minute or so of the start. One driver actually started playing the recording just after I realised what was going on; the opening line, "I was the shadow of the Waxwing Slain/By the false azure on the windowpane" chimed into the ether. Most of the others were about a minute further along. All this created a canon effect. At certain points, just as in a musical canon, the babel of voices – my own voices – resolved into a harmonic. One came as I listened, deliberately keeping my gaze at the car in front of me to prevent recognition – the point when I read "Was it Sherlock Holmes who/Reversed his shoes?" I seemed to have read these lines with particular emphasis, and a succession of explosive "Was it"s came from the stereo relay.

It's a platitude that one's own voice sounds odd, sounds faintly ridiculous, when heard recorded. My own voice always sounded gloopy and bland to me, but this canon of Waxwings did not sound like my voice. It sounded robotic and musical at once, which was why it took me some time to recognise it as my own. Or, indeed, to recognise the words as my own (as they ostensibly were), although we'll come to that later. Before I can tell you about my life as a literary success, I must tell you about my life as a literary failure.

The history of literature – the movements filled with lofty ideas, the endless manifestos and counter-manifestos, the all-too-serious sense of mission – can be considered a history of envy. Or rather a series of envies – between supposed friends and fellow writers. That has been my experience both as literary failure and success.

Since some stage in mid-adolescence impossible to pin down, I have considered myself a writer. And not just a writer, but an artist. A literary artist. The person who awoke my never-sleeping envy threatened that sense of self; because, at an age when I was still constructing elaborate fantasies of my glorious literary career, he had not only written but published three novels. And he stole my name.

The literary fantasist constructs an entire career in their reveries. The ecstatically received debut, a mould-breaking work that sets the tone for new fiction. Interviewers cast themselves worshipfully at the feet of my wit. Casual remarks that achieve the status of aphorisms. The speculation mounts for the second novel. Can he deliver? It hardly seems possible. That first novel, after all, was a stunning condensation of twenty-something years of experience and an eternity of timeless insight. And then the triumphant return, the sense of a richness and maturity that surpasses the previous work. The literary fantasist daydreams trenchant and controversial interviews that establish him at the peak of the profession.

Of course, the literary fantasist prefers to consider the interviews, the reviews, the covers, the blurbs far more than the actual business of sitting down to write. I saw "Andrew Browne" on covers and frontispieces, in an austere, tasteful font. I saw phrases like "Andrew Browne... the best novelist of his generation", blurb quotes like "another triumph for Andrew Browne" or "it is not too soon in Andrew Browne's career to proclaim him... possibly the best writer in the English language today." I even, in time, imagined the name "Andrew Browne", like JD Salinger, spurning these impedimenta of the literary–publicity complex and standing, naked and alone, on the cover of his books.

Imagine when a contemporary, and what's worse, a somewhat despised contemporary, begins to achieve literary fame – perhaps not with the hyperbolic excesses of my imagination – but a genuine fame. What's worse, imagine that contemporary has a name that differs only by a silent "e" from one's own. Andrew Brown, a writer to watch this coming year. Andrew Brown's third (*third!*) novel builds on the success of his previous work.

Andrew Brown and myself have much in common. We both are well-built, rather beefy in fact – and thereby give an impression of robust good health. We both look like hearty chaps, just about to head for a couple of steaks after a day's rugby or rowing or foxhunting. This is not an advantage when one is spending one's college years attempting to look like one is wrestling with the major issues of existence. Poets and philosophers are stereotypically consumptive, anguished looking fellows, and the literary fantasist is a great man for stereotype.

We were both members of the college literary club, under the auspices of which weekly meetings were held. Here dreadful poems on loss of faith and tepid prose vignettes of drunkenness would be read out, before the real fun began of praise or blame, carefully considered for maximum impact. Both Andrew Brown(e)s kept silent; I wrote some poems that were read out anonymously and unjustifiably excoriated. He probably did too.

I got to know Andrew Brown from the trips to the student bar after these evenings. The underlying discontent with the literary club we shared must have drawn us to each other, that and the shyness with girls neither of us ever really shed. It was a long time before me realised that we shared a surname – he went by "Andy" those days, whereas I have always been an Andrew, irreducible to any diminutive. Andy, as (for the sake of clarity) I will refer to him, was never less than friendly and polite to me. In the early days of our friendship, I saw this friendliness and politeness as fear, as symptomatic of an inner weakness. Of course, I was still at that adolescent stage (that some never leave) that confuses obnoxiousness and arrogance with strength.

Andy was generally unpretentious, but he had a small stock of what I would call "party pieces." These were declamations on some literary or æsthetic subject that he had, evidently, rehearsed before, probably alone. I heard some at least four or five times. One particular favourite was provoked by any discussion of the alleged decline of literature. These discussions are of course beloved throughout the ages – the self-selected few, mourning the unstoppable conquest of barbarism, derive great pleasure from the thought that they alone keep the flame of culture burning. The barbarians are always at that gate. Andy was rightly sceptical of this. One of the passages of his monologue concerned the trivialities the authors of antiquity concerned themselves with (this was part of an argument that any contemporary fixation with trivia was nothing new) – "the great themes – the transformation of people into animals and animals into people, various sexual positions, the glorification of whoever happened to be paying the writer at that particular moment..." Like all similar monologues, delivered with an air of authority it managed to convince the listener that here was someone who knew what he was talking about.

I kept in touch with Andy in a desultory way after graduation – an email or text message every couple of months, meeting in Dublin every four months or so for strained conversation revolving around mutual acquaintances. We both eventually started work in jobs hardly commensurate with our Bohemian leanings; he as a sales rep for a drug company, I as part of the public relations team of a major bank.

One day I got a text message from Andy, obviously not sent to me individually but sent to many, telling me that his first novel was to published three months later by a major international publisher. There would be celebratory drinks in the Stag's Head the following Friday. It was the first I had heard of a novel, let alone that it was ready for publication.

In the Stag's Head on Friday an assortment of hangers-on, people from college neither of us had seen in years turned out. I was surprised that there was hardly anyone from Andy's life beyond college. In that crowd, I suddenly realised, it was very possible that I was Andy's closest friend.

The novel was called *Sweet Science*, a solid, well-crafted story of a failed boxer's decline and fall. There was nothing particularly wrong with it, although nothing (to my thinking) particularly memorable either. While I congratulated Andy to his face, privately I felt confident that whenever I would finally get round to writing a novel, it would make far more of a mark.

With his second, *Land of Lost Content*, Andy began to garner more serious attention. It was an inventive variation on that most worn-out of topics, the coming-of-age story. It followed the conventional path of these novels – the protagonist, from a comfortable middle-class background like the one both of us shared, went to college and had the usual romantic and intellectual experiences – first love, crisis of religious faith. Rather than maturing, he regresses to childhood, which was the slight twist on the formula. There was a freshness and vitality about the writing that marked out Andy as a genuinely promising talent. A third novel, *Mercy*, a short, simple tale with Gothic overtones, set during the Civil War, consolidated his reputation. Around this time we began to spend more time together. We still had the same rather strained rapport, the same wariness. It says something about his essential loneliness that I realised around this time that not only had I been his closest friend at the Stag's Head gathering, I was his closest friend in the world.

Perhaps Andy occasionally detected some resentment on my part. There would have been a sharpness on the phone, perhaps the occasional noticeable blankness as I drifted into my own thoughts as he went on about some issue with his agent or other. On the whole, however, I managed not to show this resentment, and felt suitably guilty. There was a politeness, a formality about our relationship. I could never imagine us teasing each other about anything – romance, work, literature.

My own writing had ground to a halt. Various ideas and plans fizzled out for want of persistence on my part. Andy's success had stoked my ambition. Now I wanted not only to be published, but to stun the literary world. There was, as always, a plethora of young literary aspirants. I felt I needed to rise above them all, Andy included, in one motion.

All potential subjects seemed hackneyed, played out. I decided that what was needed was the creation of something utterly new. I wanted to write something *sui generis*, the first of a whole new genre. What is it, to create something utterly new? Something absolutely original? Is it even possible? I would seize on an idea and, in short order, exhaust it.

I tried, Lord knows I tried. I conceived of *Tyranny Considered One of the Fine Arts*, a series of essays on lesser-known but nevertheless impressively bloodthirsty tyrants.

Following de Quincey's argument – that when murder is done and the guilty punished, a sort of connoisseurship can take over – I applied it to tyranny. Queen Ranavolana I of Madagascar, Heliogabalus of Rome; such was my human material. Unfortunately, I couldn't really believe that tyranny was a mere art. Over the years, I've often liked to see myself as a rather amoral, insouciant figure, a Wilde or Baudelaire casting elegant poses on the brink of hell. Yet earnestness kept breaking in.

My other attempts to forge something new revolved around science, more particularly mathematics and physics. I read a few popular accounts of the various theories of Infinity – Galileo's realisation that an infinite set is one which contains an infinite set, Cantor's discovery of the transfinite, and his fruitless search to prove the continuum hypothesis. I conceived a mathematical novel, one whose protagonist was the mystical idea of Infinity.

I came up against the insuperable obstacle that Infinity is not exactly a sympathetic protagonist. Perhaps an abstraction can be made the hero of a story (and I mean the actual abstraction, not a personification of it), but it eluded my craft.

I moved on to what struck me, initially, as more fertile ground. Could God have created the world any differently? Could there be a world where the gravitational constant, or the boiling point of Mercury, or the laws of plate tectonics, be any different? Moving from the theoretical to the particularly, could there be a world without New Zealand, or Wlliam Ewart Gladstone or Nabokov's *Pale Fire*?

I was working on these ideas – working on a series of meaninglessly complex diagrams of the new theory of non-existence. I hadn't actually written anything at that stage. I had reached a point where writing was pointless, lacking any plan of attack – I had nothing to write about, only grandiloquent fantasies. Deep down, I knew that I was thrashing about, with no direction.

One day Andy gave me a box of odds and ends he was throwing out, trying to "declutter" himself, as he said. It was a nice gesture, though I don't think he realised the implied condescension. Maybe he did – maybe my conception of Andy as someone well-meaning and kindly who unjustly aroused my resentment is wrong. Perhaps he was really a Machiavellian manipulator of human desires, obligations and aims. I am more or less entirely without what could be called "political" guile, and sometimes tend to see it in every action of everyone else. Perhaps Andy shares this trait with me, too.

One of the objects in the box was a blank notebook. At first glance it was an old, worn notebook, but on closer inspection this was a *trompe l'oeil*. It was a new, rather heavy notebook, whose carefully cultivated look of being worn was a trick of the marketing trade. Like all writers – both real writers and literary fantasists – I have an inexhaustible appetite for the how-to tips of other writers. One piece of (to my mind unhelpful) advice that I once read was to buy some expensive pens and some expensive paper, and to use these to plan your work. By some sort of sympathetic magic, the materials were supposed to elevate your creative mind. I always thought it rotten advice, too redolent of gimcrack ideas of what's "artistic". Which is not to say I rejected it.

Thus I decided to play with the notebook. I wrote a few sketchy phrases. First some automatic writing – I set a pen (a cheap biro) on the paper and began to write "Rome did not fall because the depredations of barbarians, but fell for other reasons. It fell after some years of pain." I stopped. The automatic quality had disappeared from the writing, in my mind I had begun to try to construct some kind of meaningful sentence in my account of Rome's fall.

I wrote a few more random phrases and words. "Tubetrain. Tubetrain." I doodled a little, creating a grid, encircled by a serrated line. I wrote "Andy Warhol never existed."

Why the last, the negation of Andy Warhol? What I had written in the notebook had reflected the varied preoccupations of the time, although I'm at a loss to explain "tubetrain." There was a small Warhol exhibition coming to Dublin. I meant to check it out. I had often been in the habit, especially during boring phone conversations, of doodling phrases with an at best tangential connection to the conversation. That I should randomly write such a phrase did strike me as odd, but not exceptional. Nevertheless, it stayed in my mind.

The next day, in town, I picked up a free gallery guide. I noticed that the Warhol exhibition was no longer advertised. Unusual, I thought. Later, I looked at the gallery website. Again no mention.

A couple of years before, I had lent my copy of David Bowie's *Hunky Dory* album to a girl I was trying to impress who I had since lost touch with. Various rather embarrassed emails (one drunken evening, I had made completely unreturned advances to her) had failed to produce a response. Thus, a few days later, I decided to buy another copy when I saw it discounted. It was only when I got home that I noticed that the song 'Andy Warhol' was missing. Presumably this was some kind of money-grabbing scam, a new release leaving out one of the tracks to force one to buy a compilation. Trying to track down some information on this on the web, I did an search for "david bowie", "hunky dory" and "andy warhol."

I got no results. Refining it to "david bowie" and "andy warhol" produced none either. Then "andy warhol." None. Presuming that the arbitrary god of the Internet had struck again, I tried another search engine, then another. It was strange, Andy Warhol had been deleted from the ether completely. I tried various art sites, and again Warhol was completely absent.

I went to the bookshops, looked in directories of art and found the same result. Andy Warhol had been written out of art history, indeed all history. Oddly, there didn't seem to have been such a seismic shift in the art world. No other artist seemed to have disappeared from view, and his ideas, such as they were, seemed to have become popularised anyway. For instance it was Truman Capote who said, in 1973, that in the future everyone would be famous for 15 minutes.

There was only one source of information on Andy Warhol extant, and that was in my own small collection of art books. It will surprise you how calm I was about all this. I did not doubt my sanity, and as I still remembered my little scribble in Andy Browne's notebook, I didn't doubt what had happened. With great equanimity, I accepted that I had access to a supernatural power of some kind. It's amazing, when this actually happens, how calmly, indeed almost languidly, one accepts this. After all, it is no longer supernatural but natural, part of the world.

At first I assumed that this was a once-off, some kind of aberration in space-time. I doodled some more in the notebook, stating the non-existence of prominent and not-so-prominent people living and dead.

Gradually I discerned that some things had their own necessity, and some things didn't. Named living persons, and the artistic creations of named living persons, were immune to the notebook's power. After some more experimentation I realised this applied not only to people – I managed to negate the existence of the dodo, of Halicarnassus, of the Falkland Islands. What exactly happened to the population of the Falklands I'm not entirely sure. Perhaps there was a slight rise in the population of Britain. I managed to reduce the number of extant works of Æschylus from seven to four, but the tragedian himself proved stubbornly resistant to elimination.

What was equally striking was the fact that, while the world seemed to lose these creations and indeed creators with surprisingly little change, they continued to exist in my library. I carefully kept my eye on a copy of *Pygmalion* while negating it in the notebook. It continued to exist, but the play itself did not have an existence in the outside world (oddly, *My Fair Lady* did, "based on an idea by George Bernard Shaw", an unpublished, fragmentary outline for a story)

One day I wrote "There was never a book called *Pale Fire*, by Vladimir Nabokov." I enjoyed Nabokov too much to try and negate him, but was amused by the possibility that my favourite of his books would become a private pleasure for me. I assure you I had no thought of personal gain.

With Nabokov's book duly expunged from libraries, from bookshops, from the collective memory (it seemed) of book-lovers, I settled to read the book. It is a rare pleasure, one denied us in this age of mass production, the joy of reading a work of art created just for oneself.

As I read, a thought struck me. I had always felt that the central poem around which the work is based was itself a fine piece of literary art. It deserved appreciation in its own right. It may strike the reader as blindingly obvious now, but the sudden realisation that nothing whatsoever prevented me from publishing the poem *Pale Fire* as my own work only hit me then. It was simply a matter of typing.

The rest you know – the long poem The Waxwing Slain which was universally praised and whose enormous commercial success resurrected poetry as a mainstream art form. Within months there were numerous audiobooks, a film adaptation in the works. The imaginative leap for a young Irish scribbler to convincingly inhabit an ageing American professor mourning a dead daughter was widely commented on. No one knew the leap was via a Russian émigré author, still well-known from Lolita.

Thus The Waxwing Slain audiobook, blaring at me from all available speakers on the Goatstown crossroads. I smiled to myself at the moment, the feeling of one's fame being crowned. The lights changed and I drove on. Looking back, this was the highpoint of my career, the moment when I felt most satisfied with it all. I felt Nabokov himself would appreciate the turn of events.

Andy, who I must admit was the first living person I tried to negate, had found work on his next novel increasingly difficult. "It isn't the same" he said, "before I had seemingly endless ideas and no craft, and now I have all craft and no ideas." He surprised me by getting married. I was his best man. It was one of the last times we talked. At the wedding, I felt uncomfortable with his obvious resentment of my literary success. It was how I had been to him, I saw now.

I've written two more novels. *The Violent Bear It Away* and *Day of the Locust*. Reviewers worldwide have lauded my versatile imagination, my ability to inhabit entirely different linguistic worlds. They are a little puzzled how at my works' American setting, set in a specific time without any apparent awkwardness, or the air of a period piece. Of course, I typed those two novels, directly transcribing (occasionally with very slight editing) from the only extant copies in my own library.

But there was no joy in their creation, or in the reception they received. The moment had come when I realised that literary success as an end in itself was a sham. The elaborate daydreams when I dreamed of rave reviews and blurbs were revealed as rather tawdry fantasies. For the first time in a long time, I wanted to write a story, regardless completely of the sensation it would create, the reputation it would forge for me. I began to write this story.

And who will understand me, now that Andy Warhol and the dodo and *Pale Fire* are not only not with us, but their existence has ceased? There comes a time in anyone's life when to confess – to a loved one, in a religious ceremony, or in the full glare of the world in a book or television programme – becomes an unbearable need. I, alas, have no audience that can comprehend my acts; all will assume this is merely a clever fiction. Even Andy will think it merely a tasteless literary in-joke, so I intend changing the names of all concerned. Only I, or an ideal and hence non-existent reader, will know that this is a confession.

exile

Joel Barraquiel Tan

he secures the needle, sinks
it deeper in   the IV swings –
a clothes line – a strong wind
on the cracked vinyl stool, he steadies
himself against the metal pole   checks ids & clicks.
silverlake's sleaziest sex club – the exile

a cautionary totem to randy patrons, he is exile's
idea of safer sex education. why sink
good money on pamphlets & posters? clicks
three queens in. sex club regulars. "what swings
ya out this way?" he asks. steady
the moon hangs, a bruised pearly orb, wind

warm, summer santa anas, wind
troubling his toxo drip. i drove out to the exile
broke & lonely, to keep him company. keep him steady
through the long night. he has to work. sinks
every penny he earns on meds & bills. the door swings
open, an old queen walks out, eyes to the ground. click

another one vanishes into the night. clicks
endless scour for flesh. techno floats out, mingles with the wind
he jumps off his stool. swings
& jitterbugs with his i.v. pole to thumpthumpthump. pariah, this exile
invites me to join him, orders me to wipe that hopeless sinking
look off my face & DANCE!   he stumbles   i rush to steady

him. he pushes me off & sits back down, steadies
his breathing. a queue is forming & he resumes   click clicks.
"let me dance! if i fall, let
me." sinking
me with a withering look. he's shrunken so. the wind
could easily take him high & away from this earthly exile.
"let this bug-disease-death-thing *swing*

the way its gonna swing."
nothing to say. steady
my composure. ashamed of defining him... victim. exile
i stare at the space between the stars. he clicks
in the queens. his hair, cancer thin & translucent, sways in the wind
moon grass thumpthumpthump   drip into the needle sinks

the needle deeper   he steadies
himself but the santa anas swing him up & high in mid-click
a fierce wind   exile.

Scars

Heather Taylor

Sometimes, at night, I sing to my scars
Crossing my belly in parallel lines
The markings of your arrival
My own package of wrinkles, pus filled,
Gums wide, red and hungry
A Bermuda triangle for food then an origin of questions.

Night ritualized into stories –
I could never read long enough, fast enough,
More, more, you giggled; the one about the princess and the dragon
Head buried under armpit,
Your ears devoured what your eyes could not.

Then you were gone.

Little blonde heads, hands reaching for
Mommy Daddy Mommy Daddy
Still take my breath
Your name a weeze on desert lips.
I know you'd be that sullen teenager
Fighting over pierced lips, hair punk pink,
Broken curfews and blown-out speakers.
But I like to imagine frilly dresses and fussy bows
Waiting at home, tucked up in bed
You, before your one step behind, hurry up you
Forced skid marks
An ambulance to bellow through speed traps.

A single tone beep to silence
The end of your soundtrack.
A song empty
Left on permanent repeat.

Half mile down

Roisin Tierney

And as the bathysphere descends and light gives up her warmer hues for blue
and blueness turns to black, the sea gives quarter to abyssal forms
a half mile down. I talk to Miss Hollister on the phone, as we sink ever deeper.
We rest at full three thousand feet. Our craft's electrical beam cuts through the
dark.

Anglerfish with rows of luminous teeth maw against the window. I describe,
breathing into the phone, all that I see before me, a quartet of silver eels
swimming vertically, like arrows aiming for the moon, translucent jellyfish,
a giant octopus with an elephant's head, the pale gleam of an occasional spiralling
shrimp.

Hollister answers, garbling her words. My watch beads over. Through the windows
a light grows to twice its diameter, until the size of a penny. Some creature,
with patches of luminosity about its body, is swimming there. Too indistinct to tell
whether with or without a backbone. And then – this *must* be oxygen jag, I hear it
speak:

You have come deeper than any man before. Nine tons of water presses on your head.
Did I call you here? My nature is to attract, then disappear. I fear for you,
so brave and in so deep, and try to dim my glow. But see,
as my lure grows dimmer, my phosphorescent trail grows very big.

Here it glows a deepest pink, and swims away, leaving a trail of lights.
The cameraman sees nothing. And when they crank us up and we ascend
slowly towards the ship and they unwinch the doors, we fall onto the deck,
and I for one, (against my better judgement) am straining for a view of Nonesuch
Island.

To leveling swerve

Rodrigo Toscano

Gotta love the tools; we seek breaks or voluminous strength from such toils.

Lowdown people (we) do *not* ask when bitching a 180 turn.

The stately political beat, it will not want Holy Books, in the end, desert mummeries.

Groove into the tools, we breaks or voluminous awareness in: Art.

From corn-shucking peasant to almost all of a burgher, *spasm*.

Almighty site pattern about the beastie wound.

If the collective guilt is adapted, almighty site pattern about the beastie wound.

Them on the walkout of the Syrian Borders Bull Hides Tenderizers Dispute.

With the Israeli Stucco Bull Relief activated in phased-out lighting, diplomacy.

We as the Blockbuster News critic sentinels acting "disgusted."

Break the tools; we brinks or voluminous red runes against such blues.

E-head Octavia McKinney tied to airport parking booth, feels it (a tad).

Tweaker Rutilius Feldman tied to gallery front desk, feels it (a tad).

Whom we nodded to open a ghostly door, jacking the supplicants, one by one.

Dream that in fact is *locked-out*, to re-awake at the Barriers of Petrograd.

Play the guild master of worn monk's cowl, play the Union Satin embroidered pride of brothers & sisters.

Receiver of drummed up Class Fidelity made skeptical via optical (mainly) rally.

Tidy forms sex acts on the cardiac tidal of Wordy World Poetry.

Into the committee of Dilpey Kennedy's PAC $, extending our interests – barely.

Nice to know we don't amid wet hospital dreams of the can't afford a *dink* of a soviet.

Nice to know the about legal money frontal mutton chops etiquette.

Any way at my own peaceful DOS resistance got marked up.

Exceeding the national wound, the localist acid building, you feel DOS.

Did the DOS "postal" acting i-n-d-i-v-i-d-u-a-l mortify our courtroom spirit?

Ask the classy spread-out office exceller to post a padded sexy oval shape into the discourse.
Done to the guild's obloquy, tomatoey squishy legacy, "saucy" "retorts"

Put the McDonalds into it.

All 3, 000, 000 unassociated struggling gligs and glags.

For the Adornian leather pants don't fit so evenly snug no more.

For the Paulo Freirian *playeras* – at least three sizes, too billowy.

People what I use is little more than Kiely Garcia saves on his global calling card.

Keily Garcia, Jim Beamed straight to Channel 8, hog-tied and booked, feels it (a tad).

Who can't mask anymore what amply nests a market demand on *my* "look" – as against *yours*.

Who woke up at any-place Nevada putting a discerning eye to the horse trading all around, and saddled up half the workforce.

Gotham City Labor more about sultanate corrupt building trades subtleties than associating eager immigrants.

That lower-class seekers ply their thrusties and gyrationals against their multiple-unit owning cousins: "poethics"

How we realized our beanies were backwards oddly worn, non-abrogation of Social Contract – beanie forwards.

Mortality gets into some technical difficulties, but the you-move-I-move *meant* – lives beyond you.

I mean to say, it is *not* alive "beyond you" – it is neediest breath, the next.

The most intimate-public impulses... consciousness toggling / toggling consciousness.

The newest beanie flipped sideways – with abandon, the not back-to-front historicity.

The without the beanie altogether.

The without the beanie... *all together.*

Killing fields

Ilija Trojanow

Phnom Penh, 25/05/2002.

Wan to see killing fields, mista?
I give you cheap, mista!
Dead cheap?
Wise crack no bone.
Play the numerology game.
One million? Must do better.
Study the entrails of a dumb dog.
Two million? Better than that.
Hold your moistened finger against the wind.
Three million? Convene a round table of seers.
Silence one better than shame.
Ok, let's ride to the skulls.

In a school they gambled with the devil.
Another victory at hand,
he stood up, derision on his tongue:
You always let me win,
me, the most feeble of your excuses.

Afterwards, floating to the moon,
a voice of reason blew a fuse.
Wan to have lady massage, mista?
I give you cheap, mista!
Not as cheap as skulls, though.

Pupil

Alison Trower

I have the patience of a spider; that
black dot, its tenuous position, swinging
a little in the wind. When it comes
to waiting for the right moment, I
make a proper woven basket of it.
I build around the emptiness, always
carrying on tucking in sharp ends at
the edges of its ever taller growing sides,
ready to make my eye the lid when
it suddenly starts kicking with you.

The daisy. The dolphin. The dagger. The dragon.

Paul Vermeersch

She bites her lip, her secret, and reclines in the chair,
thoughtful of permanence, of pain, and the floral
skin of an ancestor's grandfather's father
that hangs in a museum of man.

A red-faced monkey shows its fangs, a warrior
advances through a forest of swords, and there
a wave bearing a golden ship crashes hard against
black rocks strewn across an ancient man's flanks.

The needle hums with childlike electricity, deposing
the hammer and chisel and the old ochre dye.
In her modesty she orders the cobalt dragon placed
against the semicircle of her hipbone, out of site.

The leonine mane, the plumage of unusual birds
plucked clean on an island of air, and the talons
carried under the undulant corpus, the litter
of the needle that marks her in muscle and mind.

Travel

John Welch

Earls Court, the evening heat
Pegged out between the terraces
Where tourists pitch their tents.
Walking as if to nowhere in particular
This crowd has learned to look and eat and travel
All in the one movement
But later in the Underground
Who could measure
The weight of his slack arms
Tattooed with 'England', a rose
And on each hand a spider's web?
You surface again
Somewhere north of Piccadilly.
It's quite dark now, the vegetation
Is all behind plate-glass.
Well-mannered jungle greens
Are shiny as briefcases.

Poets

John Hartley Williams

sit
on doorsteps,
not thinking
about the next line of a poem.

They go
to the seaside
just like other people.
You have to admire the way
they walk into the sea
when the red flag is up.

The surf is heavier
than Milton's
blank verse,
and the poets are out there
riding it.
If I were a lifeguard
I would certainly blow my whistle.
But there they are, the poets,
taming those foam horses
as if they were
breaking in
the metres of God.

*

Or something.

*

Later they walk
past shop windows.
Poets, the Italian suits
and the French wines
in this elegant resort

are almost certainly
worth more than your lives.
It's hardly a wonder
your language is down to a whisper.
There's so much
wry meekness
in your encroachments
on the silence:

"I have everything
I need
for my
requirements,
thank you."

What a statement!
What brevity!
What profundity!
No wonder people
simply can't hear you!

*

Poets don't say
what they mean.
They don't mean what they mean.
They don't say what they say.
They don't even mean
what they say they mean.
They don't even say
what they seem to be meaning to say.
Meaning is saying.
Saying is meaning.
Something like that, anyway.

This is unfortunate.
People are baffled.
Poets, how dearly
you would like to leap
like circus tigers
through the hoop of people's bafflement

and alight agilely
on the other side!

*

Have you addressed a poet recently?
I think not.
In fact, no one has spoken to the poet.
No one has seen the poet lately.
No one has read the last book.
Or if they have read it, they were puzzled by it.
It is good to be creative,
but what is it all about?
People play bridge, these days.
Or drive their cars at defenceless pedestrians.
Or go to the cinema.
Does one really need
to try and understand the poet
when the poet claims
no effort is needed, when the poet
maintains, in fact, that effortlessness
is the soul
of what the poet does?

*

One fears one is being hoodwinked.

*

In the cemetery
it is very cold.
There's an icy wind
powdering the graves
with snow.
Who do these footsteps belong to?
What is this mumbling?
Whose shadow is sneaking
spectrally through trees?
No, no! Absolutely wrong!
It's not a poet! It's a mourner!

The poet is safely at home,
sitting in front of a fire,
drinking a little mulled wine,
reading an excellent poem
by a dead rival.
Very soon
there's a little tapping at the window.
Tap-tap, tap-tap, tap-tap.
A slow smile walks across the face of the poet.
Who could that be?
What could that knocking signify?

The poet turns
the handle

and opens the door...

Work ethic

Philip Wilson

Crossing off days on my Poetry Calendar
I think of Ace who's spending this November
in Geneva. He bottles up his feelings
about Petrarchan sonnets while he's dealing
with the state of the AgriMaus account,
that is shaped, he thinks, all wrong. He can just about
define the company vision in eight lines
but then things drool out of control, credit loans
and expenses flooding like red lentils
out of a soggy paper bag. He tells
himself that this is the last time. Next year
it will be different. And the computer
spews out page after generating page
that he needs to digest, though critics have praised
unread collections that thudded on his mat
last Tuesday. Sometimes it seems like war.

Hotelwards by Calvinist statues
after a caffeine-led day, he's amused
by the alternative mob in DMs,
hogging the highways, making the trams
slow softly down, herded by a police
that remains unfailingly polite.
He can join the crowd when he gets out.
Write sonnets in the morning. Give up meat.
Scream at each retreating accountant
like one protestor does. She's launched
a GM apple that splashes on his shoe.
Take her away. Sometimes it seems like war.

An education

Max Winter

In the building
Spotted angels
Black sparrows by fog light
At the age of cruxes
A legacy keeper in frost
Mottled by books
Jutting out from common intellect
A flying worm in the hangar
Ready to out
Into ascending wires along the tangent
Which we will not apprehend until
The spring opened on tusks
Handmade spilling tragedies
To the left of you right of you
A triolet in the scientific propaganda ballroom
The magnetic principles explained
A youth and its phantom on tenterhooks
For which purpose was it
A fudged roman for all that

Landscape

Harriet Zinnes

Rain it is
and gorges
sometimes cascades
and of course
marshes, rivers, streams.
And lakes?

Three are mountains, too,
and plateaux,
valleys.
The crevices are careless,
and the trees are simply there.

Look ahead now
and see the cows
asleep on the grass.
Yes, asleep,
even as the farmer cuts the hay
and roses grow near the house.

Always watchful for the birds
who fly near the mushrooms,
the farmer is hesitant.
His wife is weary.

Contributors

Robert Allen

Allen is the editor of *Matrix* magazine, and a novelist, poet and creative writing professor at Concordia University, Montreal. His last collection of poems was *Ricky Ricardo suites* (DC Books 2000), and his last novel was *Napoleon's retreat* (DC Books 1997).

Tammy Armstrong

Armstrong's writing has appeared in literary magazines and anthologies in Canada, US and UK. Her first novel, *Translations: Aistreann* (Coteau Books 2004), won the 1999 David Adams Richards Award. Her first collection of poetry, *Bogman's music* (Anvil Press 2001), won the 2000 WFNB Alfred G Bailey Award and was nominated for the 2002 Governor General's Award.

Louise Bak

Bak is the author of *Gingko kitchen* (Coach House Books 1998), *emeighty* (Letters 1995) and *Tulpa* (Coach House Books 2002). She is the co-host of Sex City, Toronto's only radio show focussed on intersections between sexuality and culture.

Carole Baldock

Baldock is proud owner of three children (all in good working order), two cats (need slight attention) and a computer. Editor of *Orbis*, the renowned international literary journal of over 30 years' standing, she has written enough poems over the last 10 years to fill a drawer, and her debut collection is *BITCHING*.

Simon Barraclough

Barraclough's poems have been published in *Magma, The Manhattan Review, Poetry News, Stride Magazine* and elsewhere. He won the poetry section of the London Writers Competition in 2000.

Jim Bennett

Bennett's awards include Silver Stake for Performance Poetry 2001; Poetry Super Highway Poet of the Year 2000; San Francisco Beat Poetry Festival Competition, 1st prize and Judges Choice 2002. He regularly performs in the UK and USA, runs courses in creative writing and is editor of *www.poetrykit.org/*.

Caroline Bergvall

Bergvall has developed audiotexts, animated texts, site-specific writing, poetry performances in several languages, as well as mixed-arts performance and installation projects, frequently in collaboration with other artists. Her books include *Goan atom 1* (Krupskaya 2001) and *Eclat* (Sound & Language 1996).

Charles Bernstein

Bernstein's most recent books are *With strings* (University of Chicago Press 2001, from which 'Memories' is reproduced), *My way: Speeches and poems* (University of Chicago Press 1999) and *Republics of reality: 1975–1995* (Sun & Moon Press 2000); and, as editor, *Close listening: Poetry and the performed word* (Oxford University Press 1998) and *99 Poets/ 1999: An international poetics symposium* (boundary 2/Duke University Press 1999). He is a professor of English at the University of Pennsylvania.

bill bissett

bissett started the legendary blewointment press in 1958. He won the 1990 Milton Acorn poetry prize. His many books of poetry include *skars on th seehors* (Talonbooks 1999), which is also a recording. His poetry is included in *The new Oxford book of Canadian verse in English* (Oxford University Press 1982).

Stephanie Bolster

Bolster won the Governor General's Award for poetry for *White stone: The Alice poems* (Véhicule Press 1998). Her other works include *Two bowls of milk* (McClelland & Stewart 1999) and *Pavilion* (McClelland & Stewart 2002). She teaches creative writing at Concordia University in Montreal.

Tom Bradley

Bradley's books include *Black class cur* (Infinity Press 2001, nominated for the Editor's Book Award), *Killing Bryce* (Infinity Press 2001, nominated for the New York University Bobst Award), *Hustling the East* (Xlibris Corporation 1999), and *Acting alone* (Browntrout Publishers 1995). His writing has been published in *McSweeney's*, *Salon* and elsewhere, and on *tombradley.org*.

Kimberly Burwick

Burwick's first collection of poems, *Has no kinsmen*, is forthcoming. Her work has appeared in *Fence, The Florida Review, Hayden's Ferry Review, Barrow Street, River City, Poetry Wales* and *The Paris/Atlantic*. She is an adjunct instructor at the University of Connecticut.

Jason Camlot

The animal library (DC Books 2000), was nominated for the AM Klein Prize for Poetry. His work has appeared in *Poetry Nation, Matrix, Journal of Canadian Poetry, Slingshot, sub-TERRAIN, Quarry Magazine, The Journal of Postmodern Culture* and elsewhere. He teaches English at Concordia University, Montreal.

Sherry Chandler

Chandler is the author of two chapbooks: *Dance the black-eyed girl* (Finishing Line Press 2003) and *My will and testament is on the desk* (FootHills Publishing 2003). Her poetry has appeared in *Spillway, Louisville Review* and *100 poets against the war* (nthposition/Salt Publishing 2003).

Maxine Chernoff

Chernoff co-edits *New American Writing* with Paul Hoover, is chair of creative writing at San Francisco State University, and has published six books of fiction and six of poetry, most recently *World: Poems 1991–2001* (Salt Publishing 2001) and *Evolution of the bridge* (Salt Publishing 2004).

Todd Colby

Colby wrote *Riot in the charm factory* (Soft Skull Press 2000), edited *Heights of the marvelous: A New York anthology* (St Martin's Press 2000), and is writing a novel. His work is online at *Milkmag, Canwehaveourballback, Shampoopoetry, Rattapallax, Puppyflowers* and *Posterband*.

MTC Cronin

Cronin's most recent books are <*More or less than*> *1–100* (Shearsman Press 2004) and *beautiful, unfinished – PARABLE/SONG/CANTO/POEM* (Salt Publishing 2003). In 2004 SAFO (Santiago, Chile) will publish a Spanish translation by Juan Garrido Salgado of her book *Talking to Neruda's questions* (Vagabond Press 2001) and Tatjana Lukic is translating a collection of her work into Bosnian and Serbian.

Kieran D'Angelo

D'Angelo is a novelist and short-story writer. He studied philosophy in the Western tradition, and has travelled widely. His particular interest is South America. His current project is a novel, *Leaping Lizards*.

Robert Davidson

Davidson is the author of *The bird and the monkey* (Highland Printmakers 1996), *Total immersion* (Scottish Cultural Press 1998); and *After The Watergaw* (as editor, Scottish Cultural Press 1998). Columba was published in its entirety in *Poetry Scotland 14).* He was managing editor of *Northwords Magazine* 2001–2004, and is now managing editor of *Sandstone Review* (www.sandstonepress.com).

Jennifer K Dick

Dick has an MFA from Colorado State University and a DEA from Paris III in Paris, where she is a doctoral candidate in comparative literature and teaches at the Université de Marne la Vallée, Wice and Oxbridge Summer Programs. She has written *Fluorescence* (University of Georgia Press 2004), winner of the contemporary poetry series, *What holds* (Esteppa Editions) and *Retina* (Esteppa Editions, 2004, chapbook). Recent work appears in *Aufgabe, Green Mountains Review, Volt, Colorado Review, The Canary*, etc. She was the editor of *Upstairs at Duroc* (review) in Paris.

Andrew Dilger

Dilger's poems have appeared in magazines including *The Devil, Samizdat, Smiths Knoll, Staple* and *Verse*. He won the 1998 New Writer Poetry Competition. *Syzygy* (Notus Press 2001) was written with Robert Dickinson.

BR Dionysius

Dionysius directed the Queensland Poetry Festival 1997–2001 and edited *papertiger: new world poetry #04*. He won the 1998 Harri Jones Memorial Prize. He co-authored *The barflies' chorus* (Lyre Bird Press 1995) and has two collections: *Fatherlands* (Five Islands Press 2000, shortlisted for the 2002 Mary Gilmore Poetry Prize); and *Bacchanalia* (Interactive Press, winner of the 'Best Unpublished Poetry Manuscript – Queensland' category in the IP Picks 2002 Awards).

Isobel Dixon

Dixon's poetry has appeared in *Leviathan Quarterly, Wasafiri, The Guardian, London Magazine, Orbis, still*; and – in South Africa – *Carapace, New Contrast, Scrutiny2* and *New Coin. Weather eye* (Carapace 2001) won the Sanlam Award 2000.

Antony Dunn

Dunn won the Newdigate Prize in 1995 and a Society of Authors' Eric Gregory Award in 2000. He has two published collections: *Pilots and navigators* (Oxford Poets 1998) and *Flying fish* (Carcanet Oxford Poets 2002). 'Flea circus' is from his forthcoming collection, *Bugs*.

Zdravka Evtimova

Zdravka has published three short story collections and two novels in her native Bulgaria. Her stories have been published in the UK, USA, Canada, Germany (where she won the Lege Artis Foundation competition), France, Poland, Russia, Czech Republic, Slovakia, Macedonia and Yugoslavia.

Peter Finch

Finch was born in Cardiff, where he still lives. In the 70s he founded and edited *second æon* magazine. He ran the poetry bookshop Oriel for many years and now heads Academi, the Welsh literature promotion agency. His books include *Useful* (Seren 1997), *Antibodies* (Stride 1997), *Food* (Seren 2001) and a large selected poems, *Vizet* (Konkrét Könyvek 2003). He authors the alternative travelogue series, *Real Cardiff* (Seren).

David Finkle

Finkle is a freelance writer whose theatre reviews have appeared in the *Village Voice* and *New York Times*. He is senior drama critic for *TheaterMania.com*. He has just finished a collection of short stories.

Martin Fisher

Fisher produced and wrote the documentary *On borrowed money*. He has been published in the *New York Times* and the *Journal of Art*. He has been a media source for Fox Business News and ABC News. He is a resident at The Writers Room, NYC.

Brentley Frazer

Frazer's work appears in *Exquisite Corpse, Jack Magazine, Tiger Magazine, Identity Theory, getunderground, Paper Tiger, Short Fuse, Subversions, SideWalk*. He is chief editor of *Retort Magazine*.

Philip Fried

Fried is the author of *Mutual trespasses* (Ion Books 1988) and *Quantum genesis* (Zohar Press 1997), and selected poetry for *Acquainted with the night* (Rizzoli International Publications 1997). He founded *The Manhattan Review*. His latest work includes 'Early, late', which is part of *Poetry after 9/11: An anthology of New York poets* (Melville House Publishing 2002).

Ethan Gilsdorf

Journalist and critic Gilsdorf won the Hobblestock Peace Poetry Competition. He contributes regularly to the *Boston Globe, Time Out* and *Fodor's*, is the Paris correspondent for *The Common Review* and a contributing editor to *getlostmagazine.com*. His poems can be seen in *Poetry, The Southern Review, The North American Review*, plus anthologies like *Short fuse* (Ratapallax Press 2002), *Outsiders: Poems about rebels, exiles, and renegades* (Milkweed Editions 1999) and *Radio waves: Poems celebrating the wireless* (Enitharmon Press 2004).

John Goodby

Goodby lectures in English at the University of Wales. He is the author of *A Birmingham Yank* (ARC Publications 1998) and *Irish poetry since 1950: From stillness into history* (Manchester University Press 2000).

Giles Goodland

Goodland is the author of *Littoral* (Oversteps Books 1996), *Overlay* (Odyssey Press 1999) and *A spy in the house of years* (Leviathan Press 2001). Other parts of this sequence (Capital) can be seen on *Exquisite Corpse* and *Diagram* websites, as well as in various print magazines. He works as an editor of the *Oxford English dictionary*.

Daphne Gottlieb

Gottlieb's *Final girl* (Soft Skull Press 2003) was one of *The Village Voice*'s favourite books of 2003. She is also the author of *Pelt* (Odd Girls Press 1999) and *Why things burn* (Soft Skull Press 2001). Her work has appeared in anthologies and journals including *Nerve*, *Exquisite Corpse* and *Short fuse* (Ratapallax Press 2002). She is poetry editor of *Lodestar Quarterly* and *Other Magazine*.

Carrie Haber

Haber is a Montreal musician and writer. She won the 2003 CBC Short Story Competition, and in 2002 had stories chosen for *Glimmer Train stories* (Glimmer Train Press) and won the Scribendi award for short fiction.

Jen Hadfield

In 2003, Hadfield received an Eric Gregory award from the Society of Authors for *Lorelei's lore*, written with the help of a Scottish Arts Council bursary. Her poems appear in magazines and anthologies including *The Dark Horse, Grain, Hanging Loose, Magma, The Fiddlehead* and *Poetry Salzburg Review*.

Christine Hamm

Hamm has been published in *Octavo, Shampoo Poetry, Poetry Midwest, Absinthe Literary Review* and elsewhere. She is the literary editor of *Wide Angle*. Her book of poems *Things you can do with a sharpened pencil* is available at lulu.com.

Paul Hardacre

Hardacre is managing editor of *papertiger media* and an editorial correspondent for *Cordite*. He has published poetry in journals and anthologies including *Meanjin, Blue Dog: Australian Poetry, Fulcrum, Filling Station, vallum, Short fuse* (Rattapallax 2002) and *(Some from) DIAGRAM: An anthology of text, art, and schematic* (Del Sol Press 2003). His first collection was *The year nothing* (HeadworX 2003). His unpublished manuscript *Love in the place of rats* was shortlisted for the 2003 Thomas Shapcott Poetry Prize.

Kenneth J Harvey

Harvey is the author of three novels (including *The town that forgot how to breathe*, Raincoast Books 2003, which was on Amazon Canada's Top 25 Fiction list for that year); four short story collections (including *Directions for an open body,* Mercury Press 1990, nominated for a Commonwealth Writers Prize); two thrillers; and a collection of poetry, *Kill the poets* (General Publishing Co 1995). He has written for the *Globe and Mail, Ottawa Citizen, Toronto Star,* and *National Post.* He lives in Newfoundland.

Steven Heighton

Heighton is the author, most recently, of a collection of poems called *The address book* (Anansi 2004). His novel *The shadow boxer* appeared with Knopf in Canada and was also published by Granta Books in Britain and Australia, by Houghton Mifflin in the USA (a *Publishers' Weekly* Book of the Year, 2002) and in Italy. Other books include *Flight paths of the Emperor* (Granta 2000) and *The ecstasy of skeptics* (Stoddart 1998). His work is translated into eight languages, has been internationally anthologised, and has been nominated for the Governor General's Award, the Trillium Award, the Pushcart Prize, and the WH Smith Award.

Kevin Higgins

The boy with no face is forthcoming from Salmon Poetry. Higgins's work has featured in *Breaking the skin* (Black Mountain Press 2002), *Short fuse* (Rattapallax 2002), *100 poets against the war* (Salt Publishing 2003), and *Metre, The Shop, Gargoyle* and *Magma.* He was a founding co-editor of *The Burning Bush* literary magazine.

Paul Hoover

Hoover's collections include *Winter (mirror)* (Flood Editions 2002), *Rehearsal in black* (Salt Publishing 2001), and *Totem and shadow* (Talisman House Publishers 2000) *New & selected poems* (Talisman House). He is editor of *New American Writing* and the anthology *Postmodern American poetry* (Norton 1994). He is Distinguished Visiting Professor at San Francisco State University.

Ranjit Hoskote

Hoskote's six books include three collections of poetry, most recently *The sleepwalker's archive* (2001). He is the editor of *Reasons for belonging: Fourteen contemporary Indian poets* (Penguin India 2002). He received the Sanskriti Award for Literature, 1996.

Halvard Johnson

Johnson has received grants from the NEA, the Maryland State Arts Council and Baltimore City Arts, residency grants at the Virginia Center for the Creative Arts, and a poetry fellowship at the Ragdale Foundation. He has four collections of poetry. His work has appeared in *Puerto del Sol, Wisconsin Review, Mudfish, Poetry: New York, The Florida Review* and *Synæsthetic.*

Fred Johnston

Johnston has published eight volumes of poetry, a collection of stories and the novel *Mapping God/Le tracé de dieu* (Wynkin de Worde 2003). He founded Galway's annual literature festival and its writers' centre.

Jill Jones

Jones's most recent work is *Struggle and radiance* (Wild Honey Press 2004). She won the 1993 Mary Gilmore Award for *The mask and the jagged star* (Hazard Press 1992). *Screens, jets, heaven* (Salt Publishing 2002) won the 2003 Kenneth Slessor Poetry Prize. She co-edited *A parachute of blue* (Round Table Publications 1995), an anthology of Australian poetry.

Norman Jope

Jope is the author of *For the wedding-guest* (Stride Publications 1997), and his work has appeared in the UK, USA and Europe. He edited the literary magazine *Memes* 1989–1994, and reviews for *Tears in the Fence* and *Terrible Work*.

Jayne Fenton Keane

Keane won a 2002 National Multimedia Award for her Flash poetry. She is researching three-dimensional poetic structures for her PhD. Her books include *Torn* (Plateau Press 2000), *Ophelia's codpiece* (Post Pressed 2002) and *The transparent lung* (Post Pressed 2003). Her website is www.poetinresidence.com.

WB Keckler

Keckler's most recent book is *Sanskrit of the body* (National Poetry Series, Penguin 2003). Other books include *Ants dissolve in moonlight* (Fugue State Press 1995) and *Recombinant image day* (Broken Boulder Press 1998).

Amy King

King's work is forthcoming in *Aphrodite of the Spangled Mind*, *Combo*, *Eclectica Magazine*, *Lodestar Quarterly*, *SleepingFish.net*, *Tarpaulin Sky* and *Word For/Word*. Her ebook *The citizen's dilemma* is available at Duration Press. Her chapbook *The people instruments* won the Pavement Saw Press award in 2002. King received a MacArthur Scholarship for Poetry in 1999.

Chris Kinsey

Kinsey's poems have appeared in *Dream Catcher*, *iota*, *New Welsh Review*, *Orbis*, *Planet*, *Poetry Wales*, and *Tears in the Fence*, among others. Her first collection, *Kung fu lullabies*, is forthcoming from Ragged Raven Press.

Roddy Lumsden

Yeah yeah yeah (Bloodaxe 1997) was shortlisted for Forward and Saltire prizes. In 1999 Lumsden was poet-in-residence to the music industry and co-wrote *The message* (Poetry Society 1999). *The book of love* (Bloodaxe 2000) was shortlisted for the TS Eliot Prize. His latest book is *Mischief night: New and selected poems* (Bloodaxe 2004).

Alexis Lykiard

Lykiard's translations include Lautréamont's *Maldoror and complete works* (Exact Change 1994) and novels by Jarry and Apollinaire. He has written novels, poetry and a critical study, *Jean Rhys revisited* (Stride Publications 2000).

Don McGrath

McGrath is a widely published poet and translator of art criticism. His first collection, *At first light* (1995), was published by Wolsak and Wynn.

Nigel McLoughlin

McLoughlin's books are *At the waters' clearing* (Flambard/Black Mountain Press 2001) and *Songs for no voices* (Lagan Press 2004). He co-edited *Breaking the skin* (Black Mountain Press 2002) and his work is included in *New soundings* (Blackstaff Press 2003). He has been shortlisted twice for a Hennessy Award and was a runner-up in The New Writer Collection Prize and The Kavanagh Award.

Jo Mazelis

Mazelis's collection of short stories, *Diving girls* (Parthian 2003), was shortlisted for the Commonwealth Best First Book Award and Welsh Book of the Year.

Valeria Melchioretto

Melchioretto is a visual artist born in Switzerland to Italian parents. She has published work in *Poetry Wales, Poetry London, Foolscap, Wolf, Salzburg Review, Ambit, X-Magazine* and *Unpublished*. Her first chapbook was *Podding peas* (Hearing Eye2004).

Matthew Miller

Miller is a graduate of the Iowa Writer's Workshop. His work appears in *Colorado Review, New Letters, Open City, Prairie Schooner, Volt* and elsewhere.

Vivek Narayanan

Narayanan has lived in India, Southern Africa and the United States. His short stories have appeared or are forthcoming in *Agni, Best new American voices* (Harcourt 2004), *The Post-Post Review* (Bombay) and *New Indian stories* (Harper Collins India 2004). His poems have appeared in *Harvard Review, Fulcrum, Rattapallax* and the anthology *Reasons for belonging: Fourteen contemporary Indian poets* (Penguin India 2002).

Michelle Noteboom

Originally from Michigan, Noteboom escaped to Paris in 1991 and has lived there ever since. Her work has recently appeared or is forthcoming in *Aufgabe, Boston Review, Diner, Fence, Tears in the Fence, Verse* and others.

Nessa O'Mahony

O'Mahony's poetry has appeared in Irish, British and North American periodicals, and on Irish radio. Her collection *Bar talk* (1999) was published by iTaLiCs Press. A second collection, *Trapping a ghost*, is forthcoming from bluechrome publishing in 2005. She is editor of the literary magazine *Electric Acorn.*

Richard Peabody

Peabody is editor of *Gargoyle Magazine,* and co-edited anthologies including *Mondo Barbie* (St Martin's Press 1993), *Mondo James Dean* (St Martin's Press 1996), *Coming to terms* (New Press 1995) and the forthcoming *Conversations with Gore Vidal* (University of Missouri Press, 2005). He edited *A different Beat* (Serpent's Tail 1997). Richard teaches fiction writing for the Johns Hopkins Advanced Studies Program.

Tom Phillips

Tom is editor of *Venue.* His poetry has appeared in anthologies including *Short fuse* (Ratapallax Press 2002), *100 poets against the war* (Salt Publications 2003) and *Monkeys with car keys.*

David Prater

David lives in Melbourne, Australia. He edits *Cordite Poetry Review.*

Sina Queyras

Sina Queyras teaches creative writing at Rutgers. She has published *Teethmarks* (Nightwood Editions 2004) and *Slip* (ECW 2001), and is currently editing an anthology of contemporary Canadian poetry for Persea Books due out in April 2005.

Srikanth Reddy

Reddy's poems have appeared in *APR, Fence, Grand Street, Ploughshares* and elsewhere. He has held fellowships from the Mellon Foundation, the Whiting Foundation and the Wisconsin Institute for Creative Writing. He is the Moody Writer-in-Residence at the University of Chicago. His debut collection is *Facts for visitors* (University of California Press 2004).

Ali Riley

Ali Riley was singer/songwriter of 80s psycho-country band Sacred Heart of Elvis. Her produced plays include *dog dream, Philosophy in the bedroom, Hole in my heart the size of my heart* and *Schadenfreude funhaus*. Her work has appeared in *Geist* and *HorseFly*. Her first book is *Wayward* (Frontenac House 2003). She lives on a farm in Vulcan, Alberta.

Peter Riley

Riley's collections include *Excavations* (Reality Street Editions 2004), *Alstonefield: A poem* (Carcanet 2003), *Passing measures* (selected poems, Carcanet 2000), *Snow has settled... bury me here* (Shearsman Books 1997), *Tracks and mineshafts* (Grosseteste Press 1983), *Lines on the liver* (Ferry Press 1981) and *Love-strife machine* (Ferry Press 1969). His poems appeared in *The Oxford anthology of twentieth-century British and Irish poetry* (Oxford University Press 2001).

Peter Robinson

Peter's books of poetry are *Overdrawn account* (Many Press 1980), *This other life* (Carcanet 1988), *Entertaining fates* (Carcanet 1992), which won the Cheltenham Prize, *Lost and found* (Carcanet 1997), *About time too* (Carcanet 2001) and *Selected poems* (Carcanet 2003). Other recent books are *The great friend and other translated poems* (Worple Press 2002) and *Poetry, poets, readers* (Oxford University Press 2002).

Noel Rooney

Rooney is a poet and essayist whose interests range from ancient cultures to modern art, via European esoterica, scripture and canonical poetry, science, languages and language.

Thaddeus Rutkowski

Rutkowski's novel *Roughhouse* (Kaya Press 1999) was a finalist for the Members' Choice of the Asian American Literary Awards. His new novel, *Tetched*, is forthcoming from Behler Publications. He lives in New York with his wife and daughter.

Rebecca Seiferle

The music we dance to (Sheep Meadow Press 1999) won the Poetry Society of America Hemley Award and her poems were included in *The best American poetry 2000* (Scribner 2000). *The ripped-out seam* (Sheep Meadow Press 1993) won the Writer's Exchange Award, the National Writer's Union Prize and the Poetry Society of America Bogin Award. Her translation of Vallejo's *Trilce* (Sheep Meadow Press 1992) was the only finalist for the 1992 PenWest Translation Award. Her third collection, *Bitters* (Copper Canyon Press 2001) won the Western States Book Award in Poetry. She is the editor of *The Drunken Boat*.

John W Sexton

Sexton's poetry and fiction has been published in *The Journal of Irish Literature*, *New Irish Writing*, *Poetry Ireland Review*, *Books Ireland* and elsewhere. He is the author of one collection, *The prince's brief career* (Cairn Mountain Publishing 1996). He is also a scriptwriter and recently recorded an album, *Sons of Shiva* (Track Records).

Ron Silliman

Silliman is the author and editor of 24 books including *Xing* (Small Press Distribution 2004), *Tjanting* (Salt Publications 2002), *N/O* (Roof Books 2001), *The new sentence* (Roof Books 1987) and *In the American tree* (National Poetry Foundation 1986). He was a 2002 fellow of the Pennsylvania Council on the Arts.

Hal Sirowitz

Sirowitz's collections include *Father said* (Soft Skull Press 2004), *My therapist said* (Crown 1998) and *Mother said* (Crown 1996). He has been included in anthologies including *Poetry in motion* (WW Norton 2000), *Poetry nation* (Véhicule Press 1998) and *Verses that hurt* (St Martin's Press 1996). He received a National Endowment for the Arts fellowship for poetry.

Hank Starrs

Starrs's poems have been anthologised in *Dancing in the streets* (Orchard Books 1999) and *Oral* (Sceptre 1999). He has also been published in the *New Statesman*, *New Musical Express*, *Time Out*, *Q Magazine*, *Guardian* and elsewhere. He is a member of Oxford Backroom Poets.

Val Stevenson

Founded *nthposition.com* in a moment of boredom.

Sean Street

Street's poetry includes *'Radio' and other poems* (Rockingham Press 1999). His play *Honest John*, based on the life of John Clare, won the 1993 Central Television Drama Award for new writing. *Beyond paradise*, his one-man play on Charles Darwin, toured widely. His prose includes *A concise history of British radio* (Kelly Publications 2002), *The Dymock poets* (Seren Books 1995) and *The wreck of the Deutschland* (Souvenir Press 1992). He is Professor of Radio at Bournemouth University.

Seamus Sweeney

Sweeney's writing has appeared in the *New Statesman*, *Lancet*, *Irish Medical Times* and *Flak Magazine*. He is a contributor to the forthcoming *Meet the philosophers of Ancient Greece* (Ashgate 2004).

Todd Swift

Todd Swift was born in Montreal on Good Friday, 1966. He is the author or editor of eight books of poetry. In 1997 he was given the Young Quebecer of the Year

Award in the Arts and Education category. From 1998 to 2001 he was Visiting Lecturer at Eötvös Loránd University, Budapest. In late 2001 he moved to Paris, where he lived and wrote for two years. He has been poetry editor of *nthposition* since 2002. In 2003 he was editorial coordinator for the global peace campaign, Poets Against The War. He has reviewed for *Books in Canada* and *The Dubliner*, among others. In 2004 he was Oxfam's Poet-In-Residence. His latest collections are *Rue du Regard* (DC Books 2004) and a limited edition pamphlet from Lapwing, Belfast, *The oil and gas university*. He lives in London's West End with his wife.

Joel Barraquiel Tan
Tan is the author of *Monster* (Noice Press), and the editor of the *Best Gay Asian Erotica* series (Cleis Press). He is an AIDS activist and a co-founder of Los Angeles' Asian Pacific AIDS Intervention Team.

Heather Taylor
Since arriving in the UK from Canada, Taylor has performed her work across the country. She is the author of *She never talks of strangers* (Tall-Lighthouse Books 2003), and a new full-length collection is expected in Spring 2005. She has appeared in *X-Magazine, The Wolf, Rising, Unpublished* and *Sable Literary Magazine,* and online at heathertaylor.co.uk. She can also be heard on Resonance FM with the SaltPeter Radio Show.

Roisin Tierney
Tierney contributed to the *Virago book of Christmas* (2003), won a special commendation and runners-up prize in the 7th 'How do I love thee?' Open Poetry Competition, was shortlisted for the 2001 *TLS* Poetry Prize and received a Bridport Prize in 2002.

Rodrigo Toscano
Toscano is the author of *To leveling swerve* (Krupskaya 2004), *Platform* (Atelos 2003), *The disparities* (Green Integer 2002) and *Partisans* (O Books 1999). His work has recently appeared in *War and peace* (O Books 2004) and *Best American poetry, 2004* (Scribner's). Toscano is originally from California (San Diego & San Francisco). He lives in New York City.

Ilija Trojanow
Trojanow was born in Bulgaria and lives in Bombay. He writes mainly in German, and has published 10 books. Penguin will publish *To the inner shores of India* next year. He is working on a novel based on the life of the explorer Sir Richard Burton. 'Killing fields' is one of his first poems in English to be published.

Alison Trower

Trower is London-based poet, performer and playwright, who made her debut at Sadlers Wells in May 2004. She founded the arts organisation *LostPropertyArt.co.uk*.

Paul Vermeersch

Paul is the author of *Burn* (ECW 2000), which was a finalist for the Gerald Lampert Memorial Award, and *The fat kid* (ECW PRESS 2002). He is the editor of 4A.M. Books, the poetry imprint of Insomniac Press, and he is working on *As is,* a new collection of poems.

John Welch

Welch has published many collections of poetry. As well as editing an anthology, *Stories from South Asia* (Oxford University Press 1988), he has contributed articles reflecting his personal experience of psychoanalysis to *Poets on writing* (Macmillan 1992) and more recently to journals including the *London Review of Books, fragmente* and *Scintilla.*

John Hartley Williams

Williams has taught at the Free University of Berlin since 1976. His collections include *Bright river yonder* (1987), *Cornerless people* (1990), *Double* (1994) and *Canada* (1997), all from Bloodaxe, and *Spending time with Walter* (Jonathan Cape 2001). *Mystery in Spiderville*, prose poems was reissued by Vintage in 2003, and *Blues* is forthcoming from Jonathan Cape in October 2004.

Philip Wilson

Philip has taught modern languages. His poems have appeared in a number of magazines, and he is working on a first collection.

Max Winter

Max is a poetry editor of *Fence*. His poems have appeared in *The Paris Review, The Yale Review, Slope* and *Jacket*, and in the anthology *New Young American Poets* (Southern Illinois University Press 2000). His reviews have appeared in *The New York Times Book Review, Rain Taxi* and *Publishers Weekly*. He won the 2002 *Boston Review* Poetry Prize.

Harriet Zinnes

Zinnes is Professor Emerita of English of Queens College of the City University of New York. Her books include *My, haven't the flowers been?* (poems, Magic Circle Press 1995), *Entropisms* (prose poems, Gallimaufry 1978), *Lover* (short stories, Coffee House Press 1989), and *Ezra Pound and the visual arts* (criticism, New Directions 1980). She is a contributing editor of the *Denver Quarterly* and of *The Hollins Critic.*